# Winning the Money Game

# Winning the Money Game

A guide to Community-based Library Fundraising

The Baker & Taylor Company

The Baker & Taylor Company
New York 1979

The Baker & Taylor Company • Publisher
1515 Broadway
New York, New York 10036


ISBN: 0-8480-2000-6
Library of Congress Catalog Card Number 79-90713

# Contents

# Preface

There may have been a time when money was easier to get for libraries; but certainly, there has been no time when the subject of finance was not critical to library programs. The difference today is that the funding of libraries is vastly more complicated by the welter of federal, state and local government financial provisions, or lack thereof. This combined with the need to supplement government sources with contributions from public and private charitable organizations results in a job that can no longer be left to one librarian, a library board, or to one library friend, however powerful that friend may be.

Certainly, there are many of us who wish that the funding problem would simply disappear in a rush of public and academic acceptance, but in the long run this current focus on library finance may be a very good thing for libraries and librarians.

Money may be the coin we use to develop and deliver service, but the source of that coin is the support we must have from the political and social environment within which the library operates as well as from those many publics that libraries serve.

Find a library that is responding effectively to the

interests and needs of its public, that has carefully nurtured the support of its patrons, and you will find a library with a successful record of community advocacy that includes dollar backing.

Because every member of the library staff, every member of a library board, every member of a friends group is involved in the synergistic process so necessary to the growth of library programs, the question of finance is one that must be of concern to us all.

Whoever we are, wherever we work in the library cause, the lessons of finance point up the indivisible relationship between people power, politics, and funding. Regardless of the availability of dollars from federal or state sources, the case studies outlined in this volume illustrate the role that local effort and local support—large and small—can play in making library objectives a reality.

There is no such thing as raising money in a vacuum. As the cases in this book so admirably point up, the end result is not a gift, but a vote of confidence in the present as well as in the future.

Robert Wedgeworth
*Executive Director*
*American Library Association*

# Chapter 1

## THE PEOPLE
## ARE THE POWER

In towns and cities all across America, library professionals and friends are turning directly to the community for support. They are seeking creative ways to pay for essential information services. They are, in short, learning to play the Money Game right in the library's own backyard.

Anyone concerned about libraries knows the financial problems they face today:

- In the last decade, hardcover book prices have risen 105.6%, even more than the Consumer Price Index increase of 95.4%.
- Staffing costs have escalated to the point that employee wages now consume 70 to 75% of many library operating budgets.
- Maintenance, renovation and new construction costs have risen so sharply that some libraries have been forced to cut hours and services, close

facilities and cancel building programs.

- California's Proposition 13 has drastically affected budgets of all types of libraries, as have funding ceiling bills and cutbacks elsewhere.

But despite inflation, despite citizen tax revolt, where the Money Game is played knowledgeably, inventively, and enthusiastically at the community level, libraries are finding money to supplement their budgets. This book is designed to help librarians and library friends formulate their own strategies by sharing successful fundraising ideas.

The rapidly changing budget picture for libraries means that diversified funding patterns are essential. Librarians have heard a great deal lately about learning to cultivate private and government grant support, and about becoming political animals who know how to influence legislative bodies at all levels.

These approaches are essential elements of any successful, diversified financial strategy. But they are not enough.

The people who vote for the legislators are right in the library's own back yard. The families a town council or school board serves are the real power of the community. And local businesses and individuals are closer to home than national foundations or federal and state governments.

The community — the people who use a library every day — can make the difference in whether it succeeds or fails in dealing with budget problems. THE PEOPLE ARE THE POWER. And library professionals and friends must learn to tap this community people-power.

Throughout this book, there are some common threads, tried-and-true steps to building community support for libraries. In the nation's seventh largest city or in a middle American town, in a Pennsylvania technical college or a Chicago-area school district, in a rural southern area or a Rocky Mountain suburb, the message is the same.

Learning to manage the Money Game is a process of getting directly in touch with people-power. If a library provides services the community needs and appreciates, then there are unending ways to get tangible support.

# Chapter 2

## PLANNING MONEY GAME STRATEGIES

Winning the Money Game isn't simply a matter of acquiring funds. Mobilizing community support is just as important to Money Game goals as winning dollar support. In fact, these activities are two sides of the same coin.

Mapping out Money Game strategies depends largely on good public relations — relating the library so closely with public needs and wants that the people come to think of it and use it as an integral part of their lives.

No matter how good the library's staff, facilities, collections and services, the public must relate to them and use them if the library expects community support.

So the first move in the Money Game is recognizing the importance of strong, ongoing programs to develop and maintain people's awareness and loyalty. No matter if the community is a city, a neighborhood, a school or a university, good community relations are the backbone of grass roots financial support for libraries. If people value their library they will support it with votes and dollars.

Community-based fundraising is an important part of an overall pattern of diversified funding. When faced with squeezed budgets, library planners should look for line items which would be most appealing for community fundraising activities.

The libraries highlighted in this book draw on grass roots people-power to donate and raise money for high visibility needs, facilities, materials and programs to which individuals can point proudly and say, "I helped with that."

Slogans and catchy phrases are effective elements of any good public relations program, but they only work as reminders of the image the public already has of the library. Educating the community to library needs and services is a continuing process, building on the experiences people have had with their library for years and years.

Whether public, school or academic, a library is a natural community center. The powerbase that derives from this role should never be underestimated. Coordinating special events with local talent and resources is one of the most important strategies in the Money Game.

A cardinal rule in community fundraising is that people will be most eager to help raise money if they can have a good time in the process. Planners should always be looking for ways to combine fun, education, and sociability with fundraising.

The next five chapters are devoted to case studies of how libraries around the country have managed the Money Game with community fundraising techniques. These strategies can work as well in a small town or a large city, in a public library, a school library media center or a university research library. They are therefore grouped not by type of library but by type of fundraising activity.

Going directly to the community is one of the best ways to supplement strained library budgets. It is also a way to keep in touch with the people the library serves.

# Chapter 3

## GOING TO THE VOTERS

Bond issues are one of the most common funding sources for such civic building programs as the renovation or the construction of new library facilities. They are also one of the largest scale and most direct ways of going to the community for support.

An affirmative vote on a bond issue gives a fairly clear reading of how well a library is regarded by the people. Money Game strategies for a successful bond campaign center on reinforcing a positive image of what the library offers its community.

Though the campaign period may be short, winning bond issues is essentially a long-term proposition, based on how the people have felt about the library over the years.

Volunteers are the backbone of a bond campaign. Because most state or local laws prohibit library and library staff involvement, volunteers not only supply creative and organizational work for the election but also raise the money with which to finance campaign efforts.

Whether powerful business leaders or homemakers directly involved in their children's education, volunteers are the stars of the three bond case studies.

Library professionals and friends reading about Appleton, Millard and Dallas should keep in mind that many of the successful strategies devised in these communities work equally well when taking any library issue to the voters.

## Town Says "YES" to New Library

*Citizen awareness of library needs and strong community support for meeting those needs helped the Appleton, Wisconsin, Public Library in its effort to pass a $4.2 million bond referendum for a new building. The campaign for a "Yes" vote was successfully completed in about 2 months for under $1,700.*

In the spring of 1981, the residents of Appleton, Wisconsin, will start using their new public library — the second civic facility ever built in Appleton for a specific use. The new library has been made possible by a $4.2 million bond issue passed with strong citizen support, very little time and very little money.

The present library is housed in a converted office building originally built in 1899 and remodeled in

1955. It is inadequate to meet the needs of the Appleton Public Library, which serves its own community of 60,000, its county, and its two-county library system.

The new library will be the system headquarters, providing service for some 160,000 people in an area covering more than 150 miles. It is designed to meet community information needs for at least the next 15 years.

The pressing need for a new library building has long been recognized by many civic-minded people in this diverse community whose population ranges from blue collar workers to top corporate executives. While the library's circulation statistics have been growing consistently, facilities have not.

In Appleton, nearly 61% of the population is 18 or older, and roughly the same percentage has completed 4 years of high school or better. About a third of the population are library patrons. Because of tight space and related staff limitations, the library has been unable to develop the new programs that the community needs.

In mid-1976, voters defeated a measure to acquire and renovate another office building to extend the current library space. Library supporters felt this would be only a stop gap, not a proper solution to the library's problems, and campaigned strongly against this proposition.

In late 1976, following a complete operation and needs assessment by a consultant, a detailed program and building recommendation was proposed to the library board. The study was funded by the library and

LSCA Funds at a cost of $26,500.

Over the next two years, the board reviewed and modified the plan. A proposal was made to the mayor, who in turn appointed a library building committee.

This committee's report — and an architect's estimate of $4.2 million needed to complete the new library — were presented to the city council which then approved a bond referendum for November, 1978.

In September the library staff and its supporters geared up for a campaign to turn out the "Yes" vote. Ruth Birkhead, chief of public services at the library, was designated staff liaison with the citizens committee formed to promote passage of the bond referendum.

Because Wisconsin law (like many state laws) prohibits tax-supported institutions such as the library from participating in political activities, library staff and its Friends group could not directly campaign for the referendum.

Therefore, the "Vote Yes" for the Library Committee was formed. This group included members from the local League of Women Voters, the Junior Women's Club, the American Association of University Women, Friends of the Appleton Library and other individuals interested in having a new library built.

Volunteers mapped out a two-pronged plan to:
- educate the public that there was a library referendum on the ballot.
- convince taxpayers that it was the right time to spend money for this project.

A fund was needed to meet the "Vote Yes" committee's expenses, such as printing, phone bills and postage. To make the fundraising effort as broad based as possible, small contributions — $1 per individual — were solicited throughout the community rather than asking for larger sums from a few sources.

Seventeen hundred individuals gave $1 each to the war chest; this $1,700 promotion fund represented the entire budget for the two-month "Vote Yes" campaign.

As a means of thanking contributors for their support, and of showing the citizenry the kind of grass roots backing the library bond issue had, bookstack posters were developed for display in a local bank's highly visible front windows. Each contributor signed his or her own name on a colored slip resembling a book spine, and as the money came in, the slips were put together to represent shelves of books.

The "Vote Yes" program consisted of the following elements:

- "Vote Yes" brochures were given away at various sites, and committee workers and their families delivered one to every door in town. Bookmarks were distributed through stores, bookstores and at the library, and posters were put up in stores and on community bulletin boards around town.
- Newspaper ads were purchased, including a ½ page ad listing all 1,700 contributors to the war chest.
- Radio ads were also bought; the committee provided copy, and the radio stations made taped spots.
- The local education association mounted a smaller scale ad campaign of its own in support of the

library bond issue.

- Civic groups were addressed on library needs and potential by Ms. Birkhead and committee members. In one month, 30 such speeches were made.
- A fact sheet was distributed widely at community meetings, at the library and elsewhere.

## Media Cooperation

"Because the needs of the library were known in the community," said Birkhead, "the local media strongly supported the bond referendum. There were major stories and an editorial in the daily newspaper, radio talk shows devoted to the library issue, and news coverage by the local television stations — with videotape shot in the library."

The mayor came out in support of the referendum three days before the election. His endorsement was covered by all the media. Other endorsements came from the business community, including the Chamber of Commerce, and area service organizations.

Editorial support was also given the library vote by the high school newspaper and the papers of the Fox Valley Technical School and Lawrence University.

"It was truly a community effort involving all age groups and all areas of the city," commented Birkhead.

## Assessing Appleton's Success

In assessing the campaign, she said the short time available for the get out the "Vote Yes" effort was a plus: it focused attention on the issues just prior to the election date, and, more importantly it did not give the opposition time to organize and defeat the bond referendum.

The bond referendum carried with 56% of the vote, although not all voters cast a ballot on the referendum.

She offered these comments for other communities faced with a bond vote:

- Citizens groups are very effective—more effective than library staff or board members might have been in attempting a similar effort, even if they were allowed by law to conduct such a campaign.
- Telling the library story in one-to-one situations is worthwhile — though time consuming. Question and answer sessions following service club and civic organization presentations found questions about services, construction, and cost.
- Women were most actively involved in the campaign as volunteers — and proved invaluable in getting materials and information around town.
- The support of the political group in power is vital. In Appleton, endorsement was obtained from 11 aldermen and the mayor as well as from the full council.
- Support of a group such as the League of Women Voters — who selected the library as their project for the year — is crucial. Such a group offers committed volunteers and political know-how to further the cause.

Appleton waged a community-wide campaign based on visible and well-understood library needs. The

"Yes" vote on November 7 showed the people wanted their local library services to emanate from adequate facilities designed for the specific purpose of meeting community information needs.

For additional information contact:
Ruth Birkhead
□ *Chief of Special Services*
Appleton Public Library
121 S. Oneida Street
Appleton, Wisconsin 54911
(414) 734-7171

## Citywide Vote Ensures the Future for Suburban Branch

*When a "lid bill" was proposed to limit budget increases for Nebraska municipalities, it seemed unlikely that Omaha's Millard library branch would ever get out of its cramped storefront location and into a building of its own. But a hardworking group of citizens fought a grass roots campaign and won an $800,000 bond issue. More than 48,000, or nearly 55% of the city's voters supported a library for this area in the far Southwest corner of town, proving that community knows no bounds.*

How do you get an entire city to approve a bond

issue for a branch library in these tight-money times? In Omaha, where tax dollars had recently built a new main library and two branch facilities, it seemed unlikely that voters across town would be generous enough to fund an $800,000 building for one area. But a series of political events made a bond issue the only hope for the Millard Branch Library.

Millard, a small town southwest of Omaha, was annexed by the city in April, 1971. At that time its library occupied a converted house because Millard had earlier turned down a bond issue for a new building. With the annexation, the Millard Library became part of the Omaha Public Library system. In 1974, the library was moved to rented quarters in a shopping center to gain additional space.

The Millard area is a fast-growing community with a tremendous influx of new residents, primarily homeowners with young families. Its library is Omaha's fourth busiest.

For the past three years, a committee called Millard Citizens Library Committee had been working with the city council to acquire land and fund a new building for the Millard Branch Library. This group comprised about a dozen interested individuals as well as representatives from the local school districts, the Jaycees, the Lions, the VFW, and the Junior League.

Various efforts to obtain federal and local funds failed, and the city council told library supporters that the only way to gain library funding was with a citywide bond issue. Though skeptical, they decided to give it a try.

First, the informally structured group formed a new organization, Omahans for Libraries, and made personal requests to civic groups, businesses and individuals for contributions to fund their bond issue campaign. The $3,800 this quick plea netted formed the operating budget for an intense 2-month effort characterized by grass roots activities, a small core group of volunteers, and a belief that TV and radio ads were the most effective way to reach across Omaha with the Millard Library story.

## The Media for The Message

Gretchen Reeder, an Omaha Public Library board member and one of the leading forces of the citizens' committee for the Millard Library, was in charge of the media campaign. A homemaker with a journalism background, her primary objective was to make a strong visual TV impact on Omahans who had never visited Millard or its library, and to back this with radio exposure.

Here is how the media campaign was handled:
- Reeder wrote a 30-second "BOOK THE FUTURE FOR YOUR CHILDREN" announcement for radio and televison.
- With high school AV expert Dick Corwine as narrator, a local TV station produced both audio and visual components for the spot. The visuals consisted of 11 slides shot by Corwine and showed the library's shopping center location, crowded conditions and heavy use. A flashing "YES, Millard

Library Bonds" was superimposed on the photos.
- Ad space was purchased for radio and TV with the $3,800 budget. Nine radio spots were run the final week before the election, and 19 TV spots were run on the three local network stations.
- The press was interested in the committee's grass roots efforts and gave good exposure to them, including newspaper articles and television coverage.
- Supporters purchased newspaper ads to endorse the bond issue. A former Omaha mayor donated $300 for one ad. 70 businesses and individuals bought a large ad listing each contributor and a real estate firm bought an endorsement ad in a community "shopper" newsletter.

The committee's other grass roots publicity efforts for the campaign took several forms:
- 40,000 "Book the Future for your Children; Vote Yes on November 7" bookmark-flyers were produced, using donated art and materials. They were distributed at all library locations throughout the city (after the city legal department cleared this participation). High school civics students took bookmarks to places of business and on election day they gave bookmarks out to the citizenry.
- 1,000 silk-screened signs were made by a committee member who was running for the school board; a lumber company donated stakes and high school students helped with production and distribution. Signs were put up on lawns all over Omaha, not just in Millard.

- Omahans for Libraries spoke to meetings of as many civic groups as they could fit in during the short campaign.

When election day came, the voters had obviously gotten the message. On November 7, 54.8% of all Omahans voting said "yes" to the $800,000 Millard Library bond issue.

## Lessons of Intense Campaigning

Based on their own successful experience with bond issues, Omahans for Libraries learned the following lessons which they would share with other library friends facing bond elections:

- Short campaign time necessitates a hard-hitting, media-oriented approach to net the best exposure for the money.
- TV and radio exposure are invaluable and production costs can be held in line by do-it-yourselfing.
- Friends in civic groups and the business community are essential; in Omaha, they provided the campaign budget money which there was no time to gather by other means.
- Engage school officials and students to support the campaign with both endorsements and volunteer help.
- Volunteer power is the biggest problem, especially if you're fighting a short campaign. In Omaha, a core group of 12 citizens did most of the legwork. Had there been more time and more volunteers, they say they would like to have more in-depth

planning, phone canvassing and mailings to voter lists.

All in all, the Omahans for Libraries feel they chose the right areas to concentrate on, and they stress the effectiveness of advertising media to reach the community.

Gretchen Reeder feels that showing Omaha the cramped conditions at the Millard storefront was what really did the trick. "With TV, we were visually able to reach people outside Millard and sell them on how much we needed new facilities."

For additional information contact:

Gretchen Reeder  
5505 South 124 Street  
Omaha, Nebraska 68137  
(402) 895-2535

Frank E. Gibson  
□ Director  
Omaha Public Library  
215 South 15th Street  
Omaha, Nebraska 68102  
(402) 444-4800

## Winning Big Dollars in Big D

*Four days after Proposition 13 passed in California, Dallas voters approved a $27 million capital improvements bond program for the Dallas Public Library. Another $10 million was raised in a drive for private donations coordinated with the bond election. Added to a federal grant of some $5 million, these fundraising efforts assured completion of the city's new Central Li-*

*brary building, planned with $815,000 bond monies won in 1972 and 1975. In Dallas, individuals and business see their library as a necessary service and support it as such.*

"When You're This Stacked, You Need Some Support," the Citizen's Committee for the New Central Library told Dallas prior to the city's 1978 bond issue vote. This plea for library support took the form of posters and bookmark-flyers depicting crowded bookstacks and stacks of books.

The message was clear—vote "Yes" for Proposition 2, the bond proposal to raise $25 million for a new Central Library building and $2,040,000 for branch library sites and building planning. Some 59% of the voters did vote "Yes," and as a result, in 1982, the crowded Dallas Public Library will move to new quarters, a 665,000 square foot building in the heart of Dallas's business, civic and convention hub.

Catchy as the "When You're This Stacked" slogan and graphics are, they are only a small chapter in the Dallas library money success story. The whole saga is a long-running serial of planning, promoting, and — most importantly — building a positive image by giving the citizens such outstanding services they have come to regard their library as essential.

"Bond elections are passed based on the way the public has felt about a library for years and years," says long-time Dallas Public Library Director Lillian Bradshaw. She speaks from experience: the funding for the Central Library land acquisition and architectural planning came from two previous bond issues in 1972 and 1975. Library funds won in these elections were $315,000 and $500,000, respectively.

A preliminary estimate undertaken after the planning funds were obtained indicated the building would cost more than citizens could be expected to approve— some $40 million. Nearly $5 million was acquired in federal grant money.

To raise the remaining amount, library planners decided to turn to the people in a two-pronged campaign — a bond issue plus a direct appeal to private philanthropy.

## Going to the Public for Money and Votes

Begun in 1977, the appeal for private monies was led by former Dallas Mayor Erik Jonsson and Elvis Mason, Chairman of the Board of the First National Bank of Dallas. Working with the Friends of the Dallas Public Library, Jonsson and Mason led the Citizens Committee for the New Central Library in a multi-faceted program to both raise private funds and also educate the community as preparation for the bond election.

The private philanthropy campaign was conceived as an integral part of the bond issue campaign. In fact, many of the pledges from businesses and individuals were contingent on the public's affirmative vote for Proposition 2.

The main elements in Dallas' campaign to fund the new library building were:

• A 12-page, 4-color booklet called "A New Central

Library for Dallas." A local advertising firm donated the creative talent, and production costs of $1 each for 12,000 booklets were paid from gift money the library had received earlier.

- $12,000 – raised through solicitation envelopes distributed by 6 major banks and enclosed in bank statements sent to approximately 150,000 bank customers. The envelopes' slogan was "For $1.00 or more we'll give you 2 million books." The average gift was $5; donations ranged from $1 to $1,000 and came from as far away as the Middle East. The success of this program was measured beyond the dollars received; it was also seen as a means of educating voters and gaining their support for the bond program.
- $10 million – raised through one-on-one solicitations by Jonsson and Mason to individuals and businesses in a position to give substantial amounts of money. These direct appeals to civic pride netted contributions ranging from $5,000 to $2 million.
- "When You're This Stacked" posters and bookmarks – conceived by the Dallas Advertising League, which took on the library as its civic project for the year. All creative talent was donated, and only production costs had to come from the fundraising pool. A DPL official notes of the double-entendre slogan, "We received pro and con comments, more favorable than unfavorable."
- Display booths in the library and most of the 17 branch libraries. Organized and staffed by the

Friends during the last three weeks before the election, these displays featured models of the new building and handouts — the 12-page booklet; "When You're This Stacked" graphics; fact sheets; and "Tell Dallas You Love Her" brochures and bumper stickers from the Dallas City Bond Program, a private organization which promoted all 17 bond issue propositions.

• The Friends also distributed graphics widely and spoke at community group meetings, making low-key, informative presentations which took an educational, rather than a sales-oriented, approach. For instance, they talked about the new building and library services but did not mention the bond issue date.

Additionally, the Dallas Public Library public relations office used every possible opportunity to get positive publicity by telling the public about the library's needs. One example was a newspaper photo-story showing a leaky roof in the old Central Library. It gave the editorial opportunity to point out that construction for the new building had begun in late 1977.

Taken as a whole, all the elements of Dallas Public Library's private donation and bond issue awareness campaigns worked to get the library the support it needed. But, as Dallas Public Library staffers are quick to point out, no amount of slick collateral materials or arm-twisting can win a bond issue or raise private donations unless the library is providing services the people need.

# Chapter 4

## MANAGING SPECIAL EVENTS FOR FUN AND PROFIT

The key to successful community fundraising events is getting people involved.

People who participate in a special event for the library — be it a theatrical production, a basketball game, a benefit dinner or a book fair — inevitably find that as they focus their time and talents, they feel more personally involved. While contributing of themselves, they become more aware of the library's services and what it means to the community.

Those who attend a library fundraiser obviously contribute the price of admission and frequently purchase whatever is for sale, but they also come away with an enriched sense of the library's place in the community.

An event that generates positive publicity for the library can also serve to make friends among those whose interest and support previously seemed elusive. Even people who don't come to a special event will read about it in the paper, hear a TV or radio report — or see posters at the grocery store. As a result they look at the library's resources in a fresh light. They may come to the next library event. And they may even make financial contributions.

Managing special events is all a matter of giving people something they want in a format that will make money for the library. If the library is truly a part of the community, the community will support it.

## Basketball Marathon Scores a Hit

*Students at Johnson School of Technology found a unqiue way to show appreciation for the services of the Scranton and Wilkes-Barre public libraries. A 24-hour basketball marathon to raise funds for these institutions netted $1,500.*

They may not have set a new Guinness world record. But students attending the Johnson School of Technology in Scranton, Pennsylvania, certainly took a unique approach to thank the Scranton and Osterhout (Wilkes-Barre) libraries.

The 465 students attending the 3-year non-profit trade and technical school regularly make extensive use of the public libraries to supplement the small collection in their school library. They decided to express their appreciation in more than words by organizing a community basketball marathon with donations earmarked for the libraries.

The student government sponsored the event. While the students discussed the project for several months, they coordinated and implemented the marathon in about two weeks.

Committees handled general organization, location arrangement, creation and distribution of posters announcing the event and soliciting team participation, and publicity.

## Marathon Logistics

First, the students arranged with the local naval reserve to use its training center gymnasium. While students were covered through school insurance, special insurance arrangements were worked out to cover liability against injury to non-students and possible damage to the gymnasium. The cost for this coverage was nearly $580.

To solicit community teams, the Scranton and Osterhout libraries displayed marathon posters referring interested people to the school. About 70 teams of students, faculty and local residents signed on for the marathon. In addition, each library sent a team to play each other in one of the matches. Each team of five players paid $15 to participate.

The marathon consisted of a series of games played

in ½ hour matches from 7:30 p.m. Saturday through 7:30 p.m. Sunday. Some 1800 people attended the games during the 24-hour marathon. There was no entrance fee but students took donations at the door from those who dropped in to watch.

One popular match involved a team from Topps Chewing Gum, a large industrial firm. The all-male Topps team, decked out in women's wigs and skirts, offered $100 to any team willing to play them. A local travel agency took the challenge and won.

But the real winner was the library fund, which was $1,500 richer from the Johnson basketball boost.

## Hints for Running a Sports Marathon

Johnson faculty member Tom Krause, student government liaison, and Francis P. Dopko, coordinator of Student Services, worked closely with the student committees. They share these suggestions for running a successful marathon:

- Limit team entries to "pick-up" groups rather than organized teams to keep the competition evenly matched.
- Find a large facility, with a large parking area, to assure broad community participation and attendance.
- Encourage faculty participation — Johnson had large student participation and planners hope to have more faculty members join or form teams next year to broaden involvement and interest.
- Solicit refreshments from local vendors — to help

boost marathon profits, Johnson faculty sold refreshments obtained free or at cost.

- A marathon is a natural for TV and radio coverage — the Johnson event included live coverage from the games.
- Newspaper coverage is important, too — the publicity committee should get the message out to newspapers in surrounding areas for maximum exposure and attendance.
- Fees and pledges are the big money-raisers — the Johnson sponsors are considering raising the team fees next year and encouraging more pledges.
- Give awards if possible — while small plaques are being produced at Johnson for presentation to participants, the group is thinking of adding awards next year for overall winner, high scorer, etc.

The 465 Johnson School students form only a small part of the nearly 400,000 patrons in the districts served by the Scranton Public Library and the Osterhout Free Library. But these young people believe in the libraries and have proven it — on the basketball court.

For additional information contact:
Francis P. Dopko
☐ Coordinator of Student Services
Johnson School of Technology
3427 N. Main Avenue
Scranton, Pennsylvania 18508
(717) 342-6404

# Friends Pack Theater for the Library

*The Bemis Public Library has some very good and talented Friends. Through an annual sell-out musical revue and other events, Friends raise $12,000 to supplement the municipal budget for the library and a neighboring museum. The musical also serves to harness community spirit in a rapidly-growing Denver suburb.*

The old theatrical saw "Back by Popular Demand" is often used to describe one of the Bemis Public Library's biggest annual fundraisers. Each year, an original musical revue—the latest titled "May the Farce Be with You"— nets some $10,000 to benefit the Littleton, Colorado, Library and its across-the-street neighbor, the Littleton Museum.

This theatrical event is sponsored by the 390 member Friends group, which began in 1964 to back passage of a $350,000 bond issue for a new library in the Denver suburb. Support for the museum was added in 1974 to promote the museum's strong emphasis on community-interest programming.

The musical is a spoof of current events with a unifying theme presented in skits written, produced and acted by members of the Friends, interested community residents and staff members of the two institutions.

The revue concept originated 12 years ago with several Friends who had heard about such fundraising activities in other communities. It was so successful in its first year that subsequent presentations required longer runs to meet ticket demand; this year, the revue ran six performances.

Between 45 and 50 individuals are involved in the actual production. Participation—on stage and behind the scenes—is open to residents of Littleton, neighboring Englewood and Denver, whether they are Friends members or not.

Most of the cast and crew are amateurs. Others bring some previous professional experience to the annual productions.

"The musical is almost a year 'round activity," says Decker Westerberg, Friends president. Selection of a theme is started shortly after the final curtain falls on the current production.

Tickets are sold at the museum and through Friends. While earlier revues required posters around town and advertising in local newspapers, the popularity of recent musicals has made this form of sales promotion unnecessary.

However, publicity support continues to be generated with articles and pictures in the Littleton *Independent* and *Sentinel* newspapers, and the local edition of the *Denver Post,* as well as with public service announcements on radio and television. There are usually interviews with the director and cast members in various media as well.

### Used Book Sale Adds More Dollars

The current production is expected to gross about $15,000. After expenses for theater rental, costumes, props, sheet music and a dance band, the Friends anticipate a net profit of $8,000 to $9,000 to be used on the two institutions.

In addition, an annual used book sale (held in conjunction with the city's Welcome Western Week), an annual Crafts Fair and local house tours bring in another $3,000 to $4,000 each year.

These funds are used to pay for equipment, materials and experimental programs not covered in the library's regular budget. Six years ago, the Friends group paid for the installation of equipment to start a Dial-A-Story program and the first several months of telephone charges. When the program proved popular with Littleton youngsters, the library incorporated the service into its regular budget.

Other Friends library contributions have been a piano, which is used for cast rehearsals as well as other activities; a sound system, floor coverings and furnishings for new meeting rooms and a wall hanging commissioned for the library.

Serving a population of 33,500 with a mean annual family income of $18,000, Littleton's Bemis Public Library has some 11,000 cardholders. The revue is a highly visible and very popular community event which focuses positive attention on Littleton's library and museum and thus nets moral as well as material support.

## How to Manage a Musical

Friends President Westerberg suggests the annual

musical revue's success has been the result of several factors:

- A nucleus of individuals committed to the project and strong support from all Friends and the community at large.
- It's fun to get involved.
- Participation by individuals who've had some musical and/or theatrical experience and who can handle technical details.
- Community contributions in the form of rehearsal space, costume and prop production, ticket sales, etc., which help keep expenses down and profits up.

While the material contributions that Bemis Public Library and the Littleton Museum receive from their Friends group are invaluable in supplementing the annual budget, the greatest resource they offer is themselves.

For additional information contact:
Decker Westerberg
6986 S. Apache Street
Littleton, Colorado 80120
(303) 794-3907

## Community Barbecue Benefits School Library

*For 30 years, the big fundraiser for the Unionville, North Carolina, Elementary School has been an annual* *pork barbecue. Netting some $14,000 ($5,000 for library needs), the barbecue is a perfect example of how a popular community event can draw people of all ages together to support local learning resources.*

Every year, people from all over North Carolina and surrounding states gather in a small town 20 miles east of Charlotte to share in a traditional southern barbecue. They also share in raising substantial funds for the Unionville Elementary School.

Now in its 30th year, the barbecue dishes up 11,000 pounds of pork and more than 1,000 gallons of Brunswick Stew made from a secret recipe developed by an 80-year-old Union County resident. Families from as far away as New Jersey, Florida, and Texas have made special trips to be in Union County for barbecue day, the first Friday in November.

Last year's feast raised $14,000, of which $5,000 went to pay for a variety of library resources.

Unionville Elementary School serves about 530 students drawn from an area about 30-miles square with a total population of nearly 3,000. It is one of four elementary schools in the county which feed into one middle school and one high school.

The school has developed a strong, supportive constituency among former students, parents and area residents. It is no exaggeration to say the unifying element in this support is the community participation in organizing and enjoying the annual pork barbecue. While other schools in the state have similar fundraising efforts, none has attained the reputation and following of

Unionville's.

Since its inception in 1950, the barbecue has raised an estimated $200,000, of which almost $50,000 has been used for the library. Funds slated for library use vary each year from $3,000 to $6,000.

Allocations determined by the school's media committee help support book, periodical and filmstrip collections as well as special materials and facilities, such as student carrels, text-workbooks, furniture, and items for a teachers' curriculum materials room.

## Serving Up Food and Profits

While the event is school-sponsored, the barbecue is truly a community activity. Some 300 individuals of all ages are involved.

Working in committees, adults chop hickory wood, prepare and cook the pork in two 150-foot-long pits on school property, chop and mix ingredients for cole slaw, simmer the Brunswick Stew, prepare the plates, set up the gymnasium where the picnic is served, park the cars, serve and clean up afterwards.

Students and faculty members have a role, too. The month prior to the event, they have responsibility for selling tickets. This year, they sold some 9,000 tickets at $3 each.

Preparations start in August when a planning committee meets with principal Fred High to make duty assignments and schedule the volunteers, order the necessary food, and begin chopping the wood.

Actual cooking begins about 5:00 a.m. Thursday

morning with several shifts scheduled throughout the day and night to complete everything for the 11:00 a.m. Friday "opening," when serving begins. About 12,000 meals were served at the last barbecue.

What began as a modest activity designed to promote greater community-school interaction and generate some discretionary funds has grown into a full-fledged traditon. The event not only raises money for the school and its library, but the barbecue also is an important part of this small town's community life.

For school officials and school library personnel interested in trying a similar fundraising approach, Fred High makes the following suggestions:

- Before undertaking a barbecue, a group should see a similar event firsthand, then plan very carefully.
- Work closely with the local health department to ensure maximum sanitation and health standards.
- Order food ingredients well ahead of time to be sure necessary amounts will be on hand.
- A workable schedule for community helpers is essential so no one individual will be overtaxed.
- Publicity will be important for the first few years, but Unionville has found that as the barbecue has become a tradition, little publicity is needed. Occasionally, the school buys reminder ads on local radio but it relies more on repeat business and word-of-mouth.
- Student and faculty involvement is important but should not interfere with normal school activities. For instance, Unionville students contribute by selling tickets, which does not detract from these

young children's educational schedules.

## Maintaining the Tradition

When it began 30 years ago, the barbecue program was enthusiastically received by all — administration, school board, and community residents. Over the years a sense of accomplishment and success has helped establish the pork barbecue tradition in Union County.

Participation is enjoyable for those who volunteer as well as those who attend. A fundraising event like this benefits not only the school and its library but the entire community as well.


For additional information contact:
Fred High
☐ *Principal*
Unionville Elementary School
Route 2
Monroe, North Carolina 28110
(704) 283-4951


# Campus Theatrics Make Money and Friends

*A preview performance of a drama department play became a theater gala to help raise $20,000 so the University of Houston Libraries could buy an outstanding* *theater collection. The benefit brought in 5% of the needed funds, and generated so much good will and publicity, that individual friends donated the balance of $19,000.*

On November 8, 1978, *The Man Who Came to Dinner* brought almost $1,000 to the University of Houston Libraries. But even more important, he interested some very special friends in helping the University develop its theater resources.

This was the first theater gala sponsored by the Friends of the University of Houston Libraries, and it was such a success that others will be held.

Marian Orgain, Assistant Director for Library Development and the Libraries' liaison with the Friends, notes that the real measure of the event's value lies in the visibility it gives the library's collection development needs *and* in the contributions that result directly from that visibility.

As most academic librarians know, donors often earmark their gifts for specific uses. Thus it's very important to draw attention to collection needs which are considered high priority.

The University of Houston is a fast-growing school with a student body of 30,000. Started as a private junior college 50 years ago, it became a state university in 1963. Since then, the library collections have more than doubled to a total of over 1,200,000 books.

UH opened the new Lyndall Finley Wortham Theater recently with great interest from prominent theater people around the country. After hearing about the opening, veteran producer Cheryl Crawford offered to sell the University her collection of materials pertaining to the American theater.

An ad hoc committee of the 530-member Friends of the University Libraries was called to plan ways of financing the collection. The head of the drama department was in on the planning and suggested a benefit performance.

Everyone agreed that the already scheduled American comic classic would be an ideal vehicle for spotlighting the fundraising campaign for the Cheryl Crawford Collection.

Though Houston is an affluent city, Orgain points out that UH competes with a number of other educational and cultural institutions for private funding. Thus a fundraising activity that generates widespread publicity and positive awareness of UH is doubly effective.

By "piggybacking" on a play the drama department had already scheduled, the Friends kept their organizational work to a minimum and concentrated their efforts on good publicity. Because Cheryl Crawford herself came to Houston for several days in conjunction with the Libraries' gala, publicity surrounding the benefit was especially strong.

Both the *Houston Chronicle* and *The Houston Post* interviewed Crawford, who retired recently after a 40-year career as one of America's foremost producers.

The newspaper articles gave prominent mention to the UH benefit. They included photos of Crawford in Houston and zeroed in on her theatrical memories, such as producing *One Touch of Venus, Porgy and Bess, The Little Foxes, Brigadoon, The Rose Tattoo,* and revivals of Kaufman and Hart's *The Man Who Came to Dinner.*

Orgain notes that the primary importance of newspaper publicity was not to draw people to the benefit, but to contribute to the public's awareness of UH programs and library collections. The stories also strengthened UH's image as a community cultural resource.

Pre-gala publicity included radio and TV coverage. Public service announcements were sent to local radio stations, which announced the benefit at peak listener hours. Marian Orgain also appeared on a public service TV show to publicize the event. This was arranged by a Friend who is a prominent Houston art director, but such bookings can also be obtained by calling the station direct and suggesting a guest who might talk about an interesting community event.

The drama department had already designed playbills for *The Man Who Came to Dinner* and gave the stunning cover art to the Friends, who had 100 special posters printed to publicize the benefit. These were distributed extensively not only on campus but also to stores and community centers.

Cheryl Crawford's presence as guest lecturer to several drama classes also promoted the gala and no doubt drew additional students and faculty to the event.

Tickets to the performance were $6 each, of which $3 went to the Friends of the Libraries and $3 to offset production expenses incurred by the drama department. More than 300 tickets were sold prior to the performance, and a dozen at the box office; the total Friends' receipts were $978.

At the benefit white wine was served before the performance and during the intermission, adding to the gala ambience. The wine was donated by a local beverage company and served, gratis, by students at the Conrad N. Hilton College of Hotel and Restaurant Management.

As part of the gala event, Cheryl Crawford formally presented an inventory of her collection to the library director, a Friends representative, and the University chancellor. By that time, almost all the funds had been raised through large donations from individual friends, whose help was acknowledged in a Friends program insert which accompanied the playbills. Later, another donor made up the balance due on the new acquisition.

Though the gala raised only $1,000, individual donations pledged tallied $19,000. As Orgain puts it, "The gala focused attention on us, so that people who might not otherwise have contributed saw fit to make large and specific donations."

## How a Gala Focuses Fundraising

In academic libraries, the search for private donations is never-ending. And because of the nature of earmarked gifts, it is a very personal pursuit. Most patrons will only contribute to help special collections which excite their imagination.

For this reason, a large part of library staff and

Friends' time is spent promoting special collections so that they are appealing to likely donors.

The University of Houston's experience shows that a theater gala can be a successful way of focusing attention on special collection needs. Here are some suggestions for running a theater gala:

- Tie into theatricals already planned as part of the school's drama season. This saves on expense and organizational effort.
- Set up a personal appearance by a playwright, producer or famous actor, perhaps a home-grown celebrity. This insures wide media coverage, including newspaper, TV, and radio interviews.
- Even if there's no celebrity, talk with local entertainment editors about publicity possibilities, or have the theater department help you out. If the library helps with research, a newspaper might print an article which ties in to the play you're presenting.
- Make this a memorable social event; solicit refreshment donations, decorate the lobby — anything to insure the event is truly "gala."

For additional information contact:
Marian Orgain
☐ *Assistant Director for Library Development*
Library, Room 108
University of Houston
Cullen Boulevard
Houston, Texas 77004  (713) 749-4241

# New Life for Old Books – and an Old Book Fair

*Faced with a growing workload for its annual fund-raising Book Fair, the Friends of the Oak Park (Illinois) Public Library instituted a new way of organizing the 1978 booksale. Not only was the event a financial success, netting some $5,800, but it was a hit with the townspeople. The winning secret: turning the book fair over to a task force of nine committees, thus drawing the community together to help the library.*

It began when the Oak Park Public Library Friends Board started thinking ahead to the seventh annual Book Fair. This would be the fundraiser's first season without the experienced Book Fair chairperson, who had recently moved. After years of trial and error with sites, tents, rain, pricing, and other procedures, it seemed a shame not to continue with the tradition, but enthusiasm for organizing the Fair was low.

Reluctant to let the Book Fair fold, Friends President Eleanor Dunn agreed to coordinate the work of the Fair. She suggested the best way to get things going was "to committee it." The board agreed, and in April the Book Fair Task Force was born.

Dunn describes Oak Park as "a place where people are trying to solve the problems of living together in the modern world." The boyhood home of Ernest Hemingway and the site of some of Frank Lloyd Wright's best Prairie School architecture, Oak Park is an incorporated village of some 60,000 people in 4.7

square miles just west of Chicago. This is a well-educated community — over half the adults have attended college and nearly a quarter are college graduates — with a median family income close to $20,000.

Oak Parkers are unusually active in community affairs, and the Oak Park Public Library is recognized as a busy center of village activities. Its Friends group, more than 30 years old, now boasts more than 1,000 members who donate at least $1 a year to join.

Once the decision was made to organize the 1978 Book Fair along committee lines, every attempt was made to involve as many Oak Parkers as possible. As the project evolved, the Task Force put together seven committees: publicity, collection, sorting, set-up, clean-up, selling, and auction groups.

**Getting the People Involved: "We Need Your Help"**

The first step was getting the word out to the citizenry. This effort, implemented by a publicity committee, began in May and centered on a "We need YOUR HELP" theme. It consisted of the following:

- Mailing an appeal letter and volunteer sign-up sheet to all current and past Friends of the Library; sheets were to be mailed back or dropped off at the Main Library or at one of the two branches.
- Putting up posters in the libraries asking for volunteers.
- Call-for-volunteer letters printed in local papers.

The response was large: the Book Fair co-chair,

Marie Shapin, prepared volunteer response sheets with names, phone numbers and assignment preferences. She called each of the volunteers to notify them of their assignments as they were needed.

Just after the Fourth of July, colorful posters went up all over Oak Park calling for book donations. By using one basic poster design, the Publicity Committee reduced printing costs and simplified graphics distribution. The "Wanted: Books, Books, Books" design was printed poster-size on various colors of posterboard and was also reduced for printing on colored 8½" x 11" paper. Copies of this leaflet were available in library buildings and at local merchants and were mailed with Book Fair related correspondence.

As the poster requested, books could be dropped off at any of the library buldings, at neighborhood fire stations, or at the Oak Park High School, whose cafeteria—unused during the last six weeks of summer — was available for sorting, and later selling, the books.

An estimated 30,000 to 40,000 books were donated. Based on past years' experience, textbooks, magazines and condensed books were not accepted for the Book Fair. Records and sheet music, however, were encouraged.

During the six weeks before the Fair, the sorting committee oversaw activities in the high school, where books were brought in, arranged on the tables and stored in hundreds of sturdy cartons — supplied by a local merchant.

Library staff members volunteered to help with

some of the preliminary work, such as pricing the books thought worthy of auction. But for the most part, the Book Fair was community-run.

To increase enthusiasm for the Book Fair, the publicity committee used several techniques in addition to placing posters in shopping areas, schools, and other civic buildings. A local radio station interviewed Oak Park author Harriette Robinet to attract attention to the Book Fair. At the sale, autographed copies of her children's book *Jay and the Marigold* were sold at a special discounted price with part of the sale price going to the Friends of the Library.

Four months before the Fair, the editor of the local weekly, *Oak Leaves,* agreed to reserve the paper's front page for the issue to be distributed the week before the Fair. When the time came, the paper was provided with a photo for this purpose. For three weeks preceding the Fair, a Publicity Committee writer prepared three feature articles for *Oak Leaves* highlighting unusual materials which would be on sale at the Book Fair.

## The Big Day

Although Oak Parkers were encouraged to drop off their donations themselves, the collection committee also arranged special pickups when necessary. The day before the Book Fair, the set-up committee went to work.

On Saturday, August 19, the book sellers committee was in charge, keeping the sellers on schedule, taking change to and proceeds from the cashiers and taking cash to the treasurer to be banked. The Oak Park Youth Commission handled food and refreshment concessions during the Book Fair, keeping the profits from these efforts.

From 11 a.m. until 1 p.m., an auction of selected rare, valuable, and unusual books was held. The event raised nearly $400.

As the day drew to a close, remaining books were sold at reduced prices. After the Fair, a clean-up committee handled the final chores, such as straightening up and boxing the few unsold books, which were donated to a local church and charity.

The library secretary calculated the day's gross receipts at $6,700. When high school janitorial fees, $250 in printing bills, and miscellaneous expenses were paid, the net profit from the Book Fair was $5,800.

## The Lessons They Learned

As Eleanor Dunn notes, over the years Oak Park has learned how to streamline the mechanics of running a Book Fair. Holding the sale indoors, and in the same place where the books are sorted, has eliminated many problems, since most books are handled only once.

Timing a booksale is tricky; you don't want to get publicity out so early that books are donated before you're ready for them. With many families out of town during part of the summer, there is the additional timing conundrum of getting the word out before people have gone away, but not so early that you lose interest and momentum.

The major lesson of the 1978 Oak Park Public Library Book Fair was to get the community involved, and "to committee it." In all, there were more than 150 volunteers on the nine Book Fair committees. Of these, Dunn and Oak Park Public Library Director Barbara Ballinger estimate at least half had not previously been active in the Friends of the Library.

The lesson everyone learned is that the community loves a booksale. If organizers let the people know "We need YOUR HELP" everyone will get involved.

For additional information contact:
Eleanor Dunn
219C South Maple
Oak Park, Illinois 60302
(312) 524-0234 (home)
(312) 984-6400 (office)

Barbara Ballinger
Oak Park Public Library
834 Lake Street
Oak Park, Illinois 60301
(312) 383-5030

# Chapter 5

## BUILDING GROUP SUPPORT

$A$ s money gets tighter, libraries of all kinds are turning to formal Friends groups for moral and financial support.

An affinity group of interested supporters exists for every type of library. School libraries have parent-teacher groups. Academic library Friends result from alumni spirit or a desire to become part of a college or university's cultural life. Public library Friends gather out of civic pride, sociability, and concern for the library's informational, educational, and cultural mission.

Making Friends within the community requires an assessment of the volunteer potential and organizational skill. Once a Friends group is launched, it will essentially run itself, its members becoming increasingly involved with helping the library in a variety of community-based efforts.

Friends usually raise money for libraries, and very often friends funds are used for programs, facilities and materials which the library budget could not otherwise support. But Friends also raise a library's spirit and let the community know more about what the library has to offer.

Friends organizations invariably encourage direct contributions to libraries by providing a social base for potential donors. As Friends see what a library needs, they find businesses or individuals who can meet these needs, or fill them personally.

Many of the special events in the preceding chapter were sponsored by Friends groups. There are bibliographic references for founding and nurturing such groups in Chapter XI. The following cases look at two programs sponsored by Friends organizations.

## Friends Raise Money and Share Academic Riches

*At the University of Rochester, an active Friends group has developed varied and unusual book arts programs which bring book lovers together and raise money for the library. The events sponsored by FURL are inventive, and make fundraising models for all kinds of libraries.*

In Rochester, New York, people are proud of their local university and, in turn, the university provides a cultural hub for the community. The seven-year-old Friends of the University of Rochester Libraries (FURL), which now numbers 320 members, acts as a center of book arts activities in and around the city.

FURL began as an organization where library friends could share their zest for book collecting and aid the library at the same time. As the Friends has grown, the group has generated increasing amounts of tangible and intangible support for the library.

FURL has raised some $40,200 for library book acquisitions. It has established an endowed book fund with $1,000 life memberships — income which is used to purchase materials for the four university libraries.

And, according to Director of Libraries Alan R. Taylor, records indicate FURL's efforts have brought the libraries close to $100,000 worth of books and manuscripts. An additional benefit is what Taylor calls "the superb record of the Friends in lending encouragement and moral support to the libraries in their programs and activities."

Many members are alumni of the 129-year old University of Rochester, a private institution with a combined graduate and undergraduate population of 8,000 students and a library collection numbering 1.8 million items. Some FURL members come from the Rochester business and social communities, some from the campus. Members range from scholarly collectors to novice bibliophiles.

"We try to mingle the members' interests," says FURL Executive Corresponding Secretary Marguerite Barrett.

As with most friends groups, a wide range of membership fees allows for support by people of varying means. Students may join for $5 a year, individuals for $10, and couples for from $15 to $100; a life membership is $1,000.

FURL has evolved a policy whereby all its events must either pay for themselves or benefit library acquisition funds. In many cases, an event is first scheduled as self-supporting and, once sufficient membership interest has been shown, developed into a fundraiser.

A case in point is FURL's recent Book Collector's Seminar, the first day-long event of its kind. The program included panel discussions by private collectors and book dealers and featured a lively lecture on "Living with Forgers" by New York City book collector Stuart B. Schimmel. Held in the library's rare books room, where sherry and gourmet box lunches were served, the event provided an informal yet elegant atmosphere in which participants were encouraged to chat at leisure with experts.

Because this was the inaugural seminar, attendance was limited to 45, but the response was so great that FURL plans more in the future. Fees for this first effort only met such costs as speaker travel and luncheon expenses. However, subsequent seminars will probably be fundraisers.

## The Book Fair and Auction

FURL's oldest annual event, its Book Fair, represents the evolution of another program principally geared towards bringing book people together. Rochester's Book Fair is a dealer show, where booksellers exhibit and sell their wares in facilities provided at the UR Libraries. The 1978 Fair drew a record 1800 attendees, 37 exhibitors and $45,000 in sales for the book dealers.

Though primarily a regional event, the Book Fair includes dealers from as far away as New York City and Canada. There are always more booksellers interested than can be accommodated, so after all the previous year's exhibitors are invited, the remaining spaces are offered with an eye towards variety in price and type of materials represented.

The FURL booth at the 1978 Book Fair raised $700 from book and postcard sales to benefit the libraries. But since exhibitors were charged only for the cost of booth and exhibiting equipment, FURL didn't make additional profits from the Fair.

This year FURL expects to raise more substantial funds by charging $1 admission fee to all except Friends and University students and by increasing bookseller registration fees.

In past years, most of the Book Fair's fundraising has been centered on a Book Auction, held the night before the Fair. The last auction, in 1977, raised $3,070. Another auction is slated for fall, 1979. The auctioneer will be George Lowry, president of Swann Galleries, the largest rare book auction firm in the U.S.

## Friends as a Community Cultural Center

FURL has been particularly successful with fundraising and programming ideas which draw on local resources from both the University and the community. Some popular FURL events adaptable to other communities include:

- A benefit concert which raised $1,721. Pianist Frank Glazer, a University faculty member at the Eastman School of Music, performed "An Evening with Franz Schubert" in conjunction with a library exhibit of Schubert manuscripts commemorating the 150th anniversary of Schubert's death.

- Tours of private Rochester book collections and the George Eastman House archives. Limited to 40 guests, this popular Saturday event included a luncheon. The bibliophilic twist on the house tour theme was enhanced by having civic-minded collectors introduce and share their private libraries with UR Libraries' friends.

As another aspect on its community orientation, FURL annually allocates $600 for student Book Prizes, given to undergraduate or graduate students who are judged to have particularly fine personal collections. The Book Prizes were established not only to encourage student collecting, but also to nurture future FURL supporters.

These twin motives — encouraging interest in the book arts and encouraging support for UR's libraries— are the foundation of the young FURL group. By keeping aware of membership interests and tailoring programs and fundraisers to those interests, FURL is becoming a community asset, as well as an asset to the libraries.

The principles of building grass roots community support which FURL has followed are translatable to academic libraries of all sizes, especially to those in small cities where the university is a natural local cultural center.

For additional information contact:
Marguerite Barrett
□ *Executive Corresponding Secretary*
Friends of the University
   of Rochester Libraries
325 Rush Rhees Library
Rochester, New York 14627
(716) 275-3302 (2–5 p.m.)
(716) 275-4477

## PTA Keeps School Library Fundraising 'All In The Family'

*McKinley Elementary School's PTA raises some $400 to $600 annually to supplement library programs and materials through various activities, including a Paperback Book Fair and an annual Family Night dinner.*

At McKinley Elementary School, the library is a family affair. Parents assist in the library and also raise $400 to $600 annually, which supplements the library budget.

Located in the Philadelphia suburb of Elkins Park, McKinley is a library-oriented school, where using the library is an integral and enjoyable part of the educational process. Funds from the PTA's annual $2,100 budget are funneled back to the school library to acquire supplemental library and classroom reading materials and periodicals; add to the professional collection for teachers; and underwrite such special library activities as guest speakers. McKinley librarian Sarah Kops works closely with teachers and students in class projects, and with the library coordinating such school-wide observances as Brotherhood Month, National Library Week, and Law Day.

Two PTA fundraising activities in particular — the Paperback Book Fair and the Family Night dinner — reflect McKinley's commitment to the library and strong community spirit. As Sarah Kops put it, "All of us at McKinley — students, faculty, and parents — are one family. We could not accomplish as much as we do without the cooperation, encouragement, and support of the PTA.

"The financial assistance helps supplement our library needs. But the parents' moral support and their concern for the school is beyond price."

## The Book Fair

Started in 1968, the week-long children's Paperback Book Fair is held each fall shortly after the school year begins. The event's dual purposes are to raise money and to encourage the book habit by helping students buy paperbacks conveniently and with parental assistance.

Each year's inventory is determined late in August by Kops and a committee of PTA members. They review student suggestions and visit a local bookstore to identify new titles.

Parent volunteers then make up a 3x5 card for each book to be offered for sale, noting title, author, list price, reading level and category — mystery, sports, biography, etc. The school secretary puts together alphabetized booklists based on this information, and the lists are given to each McKinley student prior to the Fair.

Using these lists for selection and as order forms, youngsters choose the books they want and go over their choices with their parents.

Meanwhile, a room near the library is set aside as a bookstore, showing samples of the books for sale. The children come to the bookstore class by class. Parents also are given an opportunity to see the books.

When each child has made his or her selection, parents submit a check to cover the order. Once the orders are placed, they are filled from inventory, stored separately from the Fair samples.

At the close of the Fair, each child receives his or

her book order, delivered to the classrooms by the volunteer parents.

The school orders five to ten copies of most books, 20 or more copies of especially popular titles. During Book Fair Week, stock is replenished as orders are filled and supplies diminish. When demand exceeds supply, books are ordered and delivered later, but Kops says this rarely happens.

Because of its large order, the school buys the books at 20% discount and sells them at the list price. Books not sold are returned to the supplier. Last year, the Book Fair netted $600.

Some 50 parents participate in the Fair — from compiling the lists, helping students locate books in the bookstore, filling orders, collecting money and delivering the books.

McKinley students are so enthusiastic about the event that they design promotional posters, signs and decorations for classroom, school and "store" use. In the past 10 years, they have bought 10,000 paperbacks.

Many youngsters keep their lists throughout the year for use in selecting reading materials from both school and public libraries.

Every third year, the McKinley library sponsors a paperback book swap for children who would like to exchange books they've outgrown. Children are entitled to acquire one book for each one they submit. Some 3,000 books have changed hands in the three "swaps" held to date.

## The Family Night

Elkins Park, with a median income just over $13,600 —slightly above the national average of $11,500—has a population of nearly 5,000, including 28% of foreign origin. About 70% of the families and 99% of the teachers in the area are PTA members.

With this kind of interest in the schools, it is appropriate that one of McKinley's regular PTA fundraisers is Family Night. Each spring for the past 5 years, a family night dinner has been held in the school cafeteria to benefit the school library and other budget needs.

Complete with a faculty-parent volleyball game, the Family Night event draws on volunteers to make reservations, collect money, help cafeteria staff, entertain children with bingo games, serve the dinners and clean up afterwards. Proceeds from Family Nights range between $300 and $500.

As Sarah Kops says: "Learning about each other, caring about each other and participating—that's what the 'basics' of education are all about."

For additional information contact:
Paul W. Wilson,       Sarah Kops,
☐ *Principal*    or    ☐ *Librarian*

McKinley Elementary School
370 Cedar Road
Elkins Park, PA 19117
(215) 884-4700

# Chapter 6

## CREATING SUPPORT FOR SPECIAL PROGRAMS

S pecial programs are often the first items to be cut when a library budget is scrutinized. They may seem "soft" in comparison with staff salaries, heating bills and acquisition funds.

But programming is an integral part of library service. Creative programs reach out and make the community aware of what the library can offer. Programming gives focus to the public's perceptions of a library, be that a student population, a neighborhood or an urban constituency.

Special programs are obvious budget areas for diversified funding approaches.

Often, programs can be initiated with seed money

from various grant sources. However, planners must always look ahead to ways of supporting the programs after special funds are depleted.

In the following cases, two special projects have been continued in tight-money times because the community has seen their value and supported them. These same community-based strategies can work for any library committed to innovative programming and service.

## What to do when the grant runs out

*As surely as grants are given, they run dry. In Wheaton, Illinois, school library administrators began an innovative School-Community Resource Center with federal support in 1974. Since the grant funding ended in 1976, they have kept the Center alive with equally innovative fundraising techniques. It's a never-ending battle to survive, but the SCRC is doing well with diversified support and strong community backing.*

As librarians skilled in grantsmanship know only too well, government funds often come in the form of enabling grants which aren't intended to cover maintenance and development costs after a program's initial operation phase. Thus, library planners have to be ready for the inevitable day when grant funding ceases. But sometimes, a grant ends even sooner than expected.

That's what happened at Illinois Community Unit

School District 200. Headquartered in Wheaton, a suburb west of Chicago, the District serves some 11,000 school-age children in a 26 square mile area in and around Wheaton. In 1974, District 200, which is well-known in library circles for strong media programming and support, set up the innovative School-Community Resource Center, a centralized facility for extensive audiovisual and graphic resources.

Located in an old 6,500 square foot storefront, the SCRC is a supercenter which few single schools could afford. It includes camera equipment and photographic darkrooms; complete A/V production studios; such graphics equipment as laminating machines, a book binder, a dry mount press, a lettering machine, a diazo printer/developer and a sign press. The Center's professional library provides 16mm films, models, displays and educational literature on graphic and A/V techniques.

Open some 60 hours a week, the Center makes all of these resources available not only to teachers and students from any of the 22 schools in District 200, but also to everyone in the area.

Originally set up under a three-year enabling grant authorized by the Illinois Office of Education under guidelines established for Title III of the Federal Elementary-Secondary Education Act, the SCRC began with a $150,000 annual budget. However, the Title III support ended after only two years.

"It was a shock to learn we were losing our funding a year prematurely," reflects Library Learning Center Director Alda Young. "The third year was to have been an evaluative year, but we had to find ways to survive."

## Funding Sources

Orchestrated by SCRC's advisory board, the search for new funding has evolved with a theme of diversity. First, there has been strong support from community and student groups who use the Center. Recent community gifts included:
- $3,000 in profits from a fashion show held by the Junior Women's Club of Wheaton.
- $350 from a disco dance sponsored by high school students after a high school basketball game.
- $400 in profits from Central High School's combined spring band program.
- $3,000 raised by the Presbyterian Women's Group at an auction and luncheon featuring a "Yesterday and Today" fashion show of current clothes and antique costumes lent by a local collector.

Support of this kind by SCRC users is particularly heart-warming, but it doesn't come about without cultivation and a continuing public awareness program. For instance, the advisory board annually plans a Fourth of July parade float for the Center and an SCRC booth is set up at each city wide Autumn Harvest Festival.

"And, of course, the best PR we could ever get for SCRC," Young comments, "is that it's really providing the people with a service they need and appreciate."

SCRC users are charged only for material costs and certain services which staff professionals must handle, such as running the presses.

## Diversified Funding Patterns

Back in 1976 when grant funding ceased abruptly, the Center's advisory board became the backbone of its fundraising efforts. Composed of nine community representatives, the advisory board was originally set up under the grant project guidelines and thus had been actively involved with SCRC from its inception.

The most obvious source of funding was the School District. The board was able to get $75,000 for the 1977 budget, with the understanding that this large degree of support could not continue. District support has now leveled off to around $35,000 a year, with SCRC's total operating budget around $90,000.

The board also looked for foundation support but found its proposals rejected because SCRC was part of a school district. To solve this problem, the School-Community Resource Center was incorporated as the not-for-profit SCRC SHARE Foundation, Inc. This easy step opened the door not only to foundation grants but also to direct fundraising efforts.

SCRC's search for grants has been directed primarily towards small local foundations. The board feels that these organizations are more likely to be receptive than large national foundations. Though this type of appeal has just been initiated, support thus far has included $1,000 from the NALCO Foundation.

## The Direct Approach

During the past few years, the board has initiated several direct fundraising appeals.

- SCRC-designed and produced school-year calendars. Sources of calendar profits include revenue from selling advertising to local businesses and $1.50 of the $2.00 calendar price. Groups such as the PTA provide the salesforce and keep $.50 for each calendar sold. The latest calendar program netted $1,000 for SCRC.
- Annual solicitation. Using the School District list of all households within its area, the SCRC SHARE Foundation board sent letters asking for public support in the form of Foundation membership. The only solicitation costs were for paper, ink and low-price permit mailing. The first solicitation elicited some $4,000.

In terms of its direct approach to fundraising, the SCRC SHARE Foundation board feels the Center's strong public relations base and wide citizen usage are essential underlying factors and recommend direct mailings in communities where a library has high visibility and popularity. Direct mail has been very effective, and the logistics are relatively simple.

With the donations, SCRC's first mailing also brought a number of inquiries concerning, "What do I get if I give you money?" As a result, the board has decided to make a Center-produced gift available with its next solicitation.

The board advises that libraries do all they can to

win "friends in high places" through awareness of their service. For instance, Young and her staff make sure that candidates for the school board and other local political posts know SCRC's graphic and A/V resources are available for preparing campaign materials. Politicans will then have a first-hand experience of what the Center is all about.

It's a constant effort to manage a diversified fundraising approach such as SCRC's, but Young maintains the challenge keeps the board and school library administrators constantly aware of the political process and of filling community needs.

For additional information contact:
Alda Young
☐ *Director of Library Media Services*
Community Unit School District 200
314 W. Union Street
Wheaton, Illinois 60187
(312) 682-2116


# Students Find Community Funding for School Library Program

*The Oral History class offered through the library media center at Topeka West High School has generated both community interest and financial support. About $3,800 is raised from community sources each year,* *some $3,000 of which is gathered by students in direct solicitation to fund their research projects.*

During the bicentennial, Topeka (Kansas) West High School Librarian Michael Printz developed an Oral History class to make history come alive and give students a clearer understanding of their local heritage. Initial project funding consisted of a $2,500 grant from the school system to buy cameras, copy stands, copy lenses, film, tape recorders, and tapes.

The program received national recognition when it won a bicentennial citation from the American Association for State and Local History.

Interest in the Oral History class remained high past 1976, so the school administration decided to continue the program. To do so:

- $3,000 was raised by students to cover out-of-state travel, lodgings, meals, etc. This fund was solicited from individuals in gifts that ranged from $5 to $350.
- $500 is contributed annually by the Shawnee County (Topeka) Historical Society, from annual membership dues. This fund is earmarked for purchase of film and tape and to help defray instate travel.
- $300 ($500 pledged for next year) is from the Topeka West Booster Club to help with incidental instate expenses.
- Additional school funds are available on request, but are not included in the yearly budget.

## Funding The Library Class

Offered during the spring semester, the Oral History class is open to a small group of Topeka West seniors. Some 85 students applied for the 20 openings. Selection is based on individual interest and faculty recommendation.

Teams of two select projects from a list developed by librarians Printz and Patty Callison. Subjects selected this year include Georgia Neese Clark Gray, first woman U.S. treasurer (under Harry Truman); Bradbury Thompson, designer of some 35 commemmorative stamps for the U.S. Postal Service; and several ghost towns.

The program includes an all-day orientation workshop where students learn to use the cameras and recorders loaned to them for the term. A local television talk show host teaches interviewing techniques; a television cinematographer demonstrates basic photography techniques.

After the students research their topics and identify interview subjects, field trips are planned, with leave time arranged by the school administration.

The money for the trips is raised primarily by the young people themselves. As Printz explains, "We have students solicit the necessary funds, encouraging them to meet with each potential donor in person. It's very difficult to say 'no' to an enthusiastic, highly motivated 17 or 18 year old."

In addition to field trips, work is done during the daily two-hour Oral History classes.

## Sharing Community Roots

In mid-April, student teams organize their research into 30-minute slide and tape presentations which are screened at an Opening Night gala. Invitations are sent to Topeka area teachers (grades 3 through 12) and program officers of civic and service organizations.

The school's Music Department presents an outdoor concert as guests arrive. Then Oral History students explain their projects, hoping to schedule their presentations in classrooms and at organizational meetings. Following the program, parents of the Oral History students hold a reception for their youngsters and honored guests.

The 1978 preview drew some 700 individuals who viewed the research efforts. As a result, 815 appearances were scheduled during the last four to six weeks of school — starting with 7 a.m. breakfasts and proceeding through lunches, school sessions, dinners and late evening programs.

Presentations made within Topeka are free; for those outside the city, students require travel expenses. For instance, one team—which created a program on President Eisenhower's boyhood friends — filled a request from the Abilene, Kansas, Lions Club.

Completed programs are duplicated so one set can be retained by the Topeka West Media Center and the other by the Shawnee County Historical Society. Thus the students' work remains a part of the community's permanent heritage.

In reviewing the programs of the past four years,

Printz stressed these points for anyone considering implementation of a similar effort;

- Keep teams and projects manageable — no more than six projects at one time. Since the final taping is complex and time-consuming, more than six projects impinge on other library work.
- Ensure a "line" item in the school budget for the project if possible.
- Involve students in all aspects of the effort, from identifying resources to making their own travel arrangements. This enhances the learning experience.
- Encourage parents and teachers to get involved by suggesting potential community donors.
- Special community-based projects attract good media coverage, which in turn attracts contributions. The Oral History class previews brought media interviews of both subjects and students.

The Topeka West Oral History class is an excellent example of a special library project made possible by student fundraising in a receptive community. The research presentations are a focus for community interest and pride, a model of what a creative library media center can accomplish.

For additional information contact:
Michael Printz
Topeka West High School
2001 Fairlawn Road
Topeka, Kansas 66604
(913) 272-1634

# Chapter 7

## RETAILING AT THE LIBRARY

In recent years, innovation has become the key to library survival. In addition to used book sales, bond issues, and other such familiar techniques, budget-wise administrators are increasingly turning to another source for expanded library income — retailing.

Some libraries sell notepaper and prints of local scenery or treasures from their own collections. Some sell Christmas cards and gift books. Others offer paperbacks.

A library store may be run by volunteers or staff members. The shop may be a small display area in the corner of an entrance hall or a separate room. Whichever, the merchandise and sales strategy must be tailored to each particular library situation.

The following case and the "Variety In Store" section of chapter 8 show what it takes to run a successful merchandising program: imagination, planning and —

as with any sales operation—an understanding of what people need and want.

The net profit can be a satisfied library community and a boost for the library budget.

## Selling Books and Service at the Library

*Community-focused activities of the Hingham, Massachusetts, Public Library have resulted in several creative merchandising programs. Book rental proceeds of $5,000 finance Hingham's bookstore, which generates a profit of about $1,500 annually.*

At the Hingham, Massachusetts, Public Library, a bookstore in the lobby sells paperbacks year 'round and offers a wide selection of gift books for sale at Christmas. This retailing program is financed with book rental proceeds and nets the library some $1,500 each year.

The funds derived from selling books are a useful addition to the library's budget. But making money wasn't the primary motive in setting up the bookstore when it opened 12 years ago. Instead, in Hingham, the idea of offering books for sale is just one more way of making the library the best resource and information center in town.

Hingham is a 22 square mile suburb about 15 miles south of Boston. Its 20,000 residents are relatively affluent—with a median income 31.5% above that of

Boston — and well-educated — 26% have completed college. When the Hingham Public Library moved into a new building in 1966, a paperback bookstore seemed a natural addition to the library's services.

This same emphasis on service was the basis of a bestseller rental collection started by the library's Friends group 20 years ago and now managed by Hingham Director Walter Dziura. Rental charges are a nickel a day and books stay in circulation as long as they're in demand — sometimes for as long as a year.

When demand declines, the books are transferred to the general collection. The $5,000 annual rental collection proceeds provide the operating funds for the library bookstore to buy its stock.

**The Library Bookstore**

Consisting of three or four racks of 100 paperbacks each, the bookshop features all subjects, with emphasis on popular fiction, cookbooks, sports and dictionaries.

The library buys these books from paperback distributors and other wholesalers serving the library. It then sells the books at 10% off list price. Stock is replenished periodically as necessary.

For the Christmas season, the selection is widened to include hardcover and gift selections on such topics as sailing, gardening, crafts, and children's interests. The larger holiday stock is displayed on long tables adjacent to the racks.

Dziura comments that most of the bookstore sales are the result of impulse buying. Some $1,100 is generated during the Christmas season, and $300 to $400 the rest of the year. Hingham Public Library sells about 1,000 books a year.

Unsold paperbacks are cataloged and transferred to the loan collection. Patrons interested in reading—but not owning — a title in the bookstore are accommodated by cataloging and loaning out the books they choose. On occasion, if a patron wants to buy a book that cannot be obtained through a regular bookstore, the library will place a special order.

Based on his library's experience in the bookstore business, Dziura offers the following guidelines for setting up a successful bookshop:

- Limit selections to popular reading and books of special interest to community residents. Dziura hand-picked all the titles at the beginning, but this proved time consuming and unnecessary. Now, he simply selects a variety of paperbacks on popular topics.

- Keep duplicates of titles to a minimum—the wider the range, the more likely a title will appeal to an impulse buyer. Duplicate only highly popular books with a mass appeal.

- Plan to keep the books. This reduces the need for inventory control, and paperwork for returning books.

- Select titles with a general adult audience in mind. While the Hingham library does include children's books for Christmas, as a rule parents are dissatisfied with the quality and price of children's paperbacks.

- Have the paperbacks easily accessible to patrons and let them make their selections at leisure. At Hingham, the racks are in the lobby near the main desk. No staff person is assigned to monitor the area. After selections are made they can be paid for at the desk. Losses have been minimal.
- Consider the bookstore primarily as another service of the library rather than a major fundraising activity.

Hingham also has other sources for discretionary funds which arise from its concept of broad-based community service:

- Beverage and candy sales in the adult browsing room. These bring in some $300 a year and lots of community goodwill. In addition, Dziura notes, they tend to increase usage by encouraging people to stay in the library longer.
- Rental fees for special nonprint materials. Hingham loans a number of unusual items, including portable electric typewriters, acoustic guitars, sewing machines, telescopes, 8mm film projectors, cassette players and cassettes. There is a small daily charge for some of these items, to help defray the costs of maintenance and repair.

Circulating more than 315,000 books annually — an average of nearly 16 books per resident — the library has one of the highest user rates for libraries of its size in Massachusetts. This success is attributable to the same broad service philosophy that gave rise to its sales and rental programs.

The Hingham Public Library has shown its community that the library is a place which loans books and meets a variety of special needs.

For additional information contact:
Walter T. Dziura
□ *Director*
Hingham Public Library
66 Leavitt Street
Hingham, Massachusetts 02043
(617) 749-0907

# Chapter 8

## MORE WINNING IDEAS ... IN BRIEF

Libraries have many supporters — well-organized Friends and Associates groups; concerned individuals, and, of course, patrons.

Whether participating in a coordinated year 'round program or forming an ad hoc group for special projects, these supporters benefit a library in two very important ways:

- They expand a library's budget by tapping community sources for funds and volunteer assistance.
- They bring the library's message into the community, generating goodwill and fostering a positive climate for library votes and fundraising activities.

The ideas briefly reviewed in this section illustrate creative, successful ways friends of public, school and academic libraries have built community goodwill while generating discretionary funds for library use.

Projects range from book sales to bank promotions. Some are quick, easy to accomplish while others require months of extensive, coordinated effort on the part of volunteers and library staff.

All proved successful both in meeting financial goals and in improving community appreciation for and awareness of the library's special role in citizens' lives.

The common element in these projects is commitment — on the part of supporters, library personnel, and the community at large.

For detailed information on a specific fundraising effort, contact the library cited.

## BUSINESS COOPERATION

The business community has proven helpful to many libraries in the way of "in-kind" service as well as grants and financial contributions. However, some libraries have implemented cooperative programs with businesses which have generated third-party financial gifts.

### Bank Promotions

The New York Public Library developed a fundraising program with branches of the East New York Savings Bank. During a three week period, new bank depositors could waive their premium, and the value of the item was donated to the library. The bank then matched each contribution to the fund. Each contributor received a certificate of recognition; bookplates with the names of the donors were placed in books purchased with the funds.

The promotion brought the library $25,000 — $10,000 from depositors; $10,000 in matching bank funds; and $5,000 contributed by bank executives. The promotion also generated widespread publicity, further promoting the library.

### Savers Support Libraries

A slightly different version of a bank/library promotion was conducted by 16 Atlantic National Banks in five Florida counties to benefit 250 public, private, school and college libraries. The "You're Overdue at the Library" promotion ran for six weeks during which time the banks donated $4 for each new savings account of $100 or more as well as for each $100 or more deposited to an existing account.

The promotion was advertised in newspapers, through handout sheets, on radio and television as well as through bookmarks, stuffers, and posters. The Jacksonville Public Library staffed a week-long display in one bank, distributing service brochures and bookmarks.

Depositors could designate a branch, school or academic library as recipient of the bank contributions. Bookplates with names of individual donors were pasted into new volumes acquired with the funds. The promotion netted $9,160, with about 25% of that designated for the Jacksonville Public Library System.

## Mall Library

Children in Oakville, Ontario (Canada) are getting their own library—a medieval castle—built as part of a privately developed children's village housing some 40 specialty shops, professional offices, and other businesses geared to the young audience. The developer will lease the land from the city and turn the new facility over to the Library Board for a $1 annual rental.

The idea was sparked by Stan Squires, director of children's services for the Oakville Public Library, to meet the growing need for children's services. The library, being built at no cost to taxpayers, will be the focal point of the complex.

## BANKING ON BOOKS

Book related events, such as sales, have long been popular with libraries. The following are some variations on the book sale that have proved successful.

### Book Appraisal Clinic

Friends of the Malcolm Love Library (San Diego, California, State University) sponsored a two-day book appraisal clinic. Four expert appraisers from the area evaluated volumes brought in by Friends members, students and members of the community. A schedule of fees was set up ranging from $5 for a single volume to $12 for sets of up to 4 books. Friends members were given a discount.

Some appraisers received a stipend for their efforts, others donated their services. Several hundred dollars were raised for the Friends general funds.

## Book Shower

To increase its book budget, the Public Library of Johnston County and Smithfield (North Carolina) conducted a "Book Shower" during National Library Week. The library sent about 2,400 letters to patrons, businesses and industries, and civic groups in the community at a cost of nearly $80 in postage and materials. The first appeal raised $1,395; a second appeal brought in $1,692. Funds were used for the library's book collection.

## Book Fair

Book fairs and sales are popular fundraising activities with all kind of libraries.

The Marin Country Day School (Corte Madera, California) has sponsored an annual new book fair for the past 22 years. Parent volunteers check book reviews, consult bookstores and monitor the school's microfiche system to select the 800 or so titles that will be available at the week-long fair.

Display copies and some paperbacks for a "cash and carry" table are purchased for the fair from the school's wholesalers. Once the fair begins, book buyers fill in specially printed order cards. Multiple copies are then ordered from the same wholesalers. The parent group uses a resale number and takes advantage of the wholesalers' discount schedule.

This year the fair grossed $20,000 with a net profit of $5,500 for the school library.

## Used Book Sale

Another long standing book sale is sponsored by members of the Brandeis University National Women's Committee. About 45 or 50 sales are conducted throughout the country at various times of the year.

One of the largest sales is held each May in Wilmette, a Chicago suburb, where book buyers from the metropolitan Chicago area can select from some 300,000 used books offered in 40 categories.

The Wilmette sale, now in its 20th year, includes a closed bid auction of signed first editions, limited editions and rare and valuable items. Sales in other areas offer memorabilia, records and art objects.

## History Book

A bicentennial-inspired project has become a long-term fundraising effort for the Baltimore County Public Library (Towson, Maryland). The county's bicentennial committee advanced funds for *A History of Baltimore County* to be written by historians at two local academic institutions. This developed into a 555-page book updating a previous history issued in 1888. The Friends of the Baltimore County Public Library agreed to underwrite the $15,000 printing costs from funds earmarked for special projects.

An initial press run of 4,900 was ordered, with

books priced at $15.95 and available through area bookstores, gift and card shops and library branches.

Proceeds from the sale — after recouping expenses — will be used by the Friends group to meet various library needs. The Friends have already allocated $3,000 for library programs for the coming year.

## Wheelbarrow Campaign

A piece of library lore sparked fundraising efforts at the Samford University library (Birmingham, Alabama). Theme of the Project Wheelbarrow fund and book drive symbolizes an 1841 effort by the University's first president to solicit donations by pushing a wheelbarrow through the streets.

The current campaign involved an appeal letter sent to previous donors, library patrons and other potential contributors. The library sought both funds and books.

Art showing current librarian F. Wilbur Helmbold pushing a book-laden wheelbarrow was designed for bookplates and staff T-shirts. A library display featuring a wheelbarrow further drew attention to the campaign.

Among the contributions was a collection of John Masefield works covering his early years. In addition, the nearly $6,000 raised during the campaign enabled the library to purchase a Masefield collection covering the later part of his life. Thus, the Samford University library now has a distinguished first edition collection made possible through Project Wheelbarrow.

Other paperback contributions have come from library patrons, and on occasion, there will be hardcover books.

The library displays the books on shelves in its hallway; patrons make their own selections and pay for their purchases at the circulation desk.

## VARIETY 'IN STORE' AT THE LIBRARY

A growing number of libraries are establishing retail operations. Merchandise varies from used books to postcards, maps and guides. One library maintains a thrift shop. Volunteers staff these operations which range from a lobby corner to a complete shop.

### Thrift Shop

The Ketchum/Sun Valley Community Library (Ketchum, Idaho) is unique in a number of ways. Completely financed through private sources, the library has "The Gold Mine" to help supplement its annual budget. Started 24 years ago, "The Gold Mine" is a thrift shop operated Tuesday through Saturday, six hours each day. Staff includes one salaried salesclerk and volunteers who donate about 2700 hours annually.

Items for sale include clothing and furniture contributed by permanent and summer residents. The thrift shop profits, supplemented by private donations and proceeds from a home tour and tennis tournament, provide the library's budget.

Now in its second year, the paperback book operation was started by librarian Wallace Houk after a chance meeting with the owner of the paperback bookstore.

Variations of the bookstore concept have been implemented by Friends groups at the public libraries in Columbus, Ohio, and Minneapolis, Minnesota.

## Paperback Sales

Thousands of used paperbacks are being recycled each year by the Alvin Community College Library (Alvin, Texas). The library receives some 5,500 free used paperbacks several times a year from a local bookstore owner who's received them in trade for new books. The library sells the books for 10 cents each — which increases its book budget by $900 to $1,200 annually.

## Used Books

The Columbus store, Secondhand Prose, specializes in used paperbacks and hardcover books weeded from the library's collection and donated by the public. Occasionally the store offers records, sheet music, periodicals and new book donations the library does not choose to keep. Sheet music and periodicals have been especially popular.

Opened about two years ago, Secondhand Prose rents the shop, an office and supply room in the main library for a nominal annual fee. Friends volunteers staff the store from 10 a.m. to 3 p.m. Mondays, Thursdays and Fridays, and from 5 to 7:30 p.m. Thursdays. The Friends acquire books for the store through a public lot bid to the library (required by state law) then resell them to the public. The last bid covers the next five years. The store was opened as an ongoing fundraiser in response to the success of the semi-annual book sales held in the library's bookmobile garage.

Secondhand Prose brings the library about $3,600 annually which is used for programming, children's summer reading, adult and volunteer services, and opening various exhibitions. The book sales add between $4,000 and $6,000 to library funds depending on book inventory.

All books sold by the Columbus Public Library Friends — at the sales and in the store — are priced 15¢ for paperbacks and 35¢ for hardcovers (prices had been 10¢ and 25¢ until April). Special offers — such as encyclopedia sets — are sold through closed bid.

Friends chapters at the branch libraries can also conduct book sales drawing stock from the central source. Funds generated locally are used for branch programs.

New books are sometimes available through autographing programs such as a wine and cheese party held for Alex Haley.

### Local Interest Items

The Minneapolis store, about 5 years old, is currently located at an unused checkout counter in the lobby of the main library. The shop is staffed by

Friends and offers new books, cards, maps, guidebooks, and calendars on topics of Minnesota interest.

Volunteers work in half-day shifts, five days a week (10 a.m. to 3 p.m.), during peak library traffic hours. Friends buy books from a local supplier at normal retail discount and resell at list price. Except for especially popular items or closeouts, stock is kept small because of limited storage space.

The operation nets about $4,000 each year for the Friends general fund. In addition to fundraising, Friends see the book shop as a public relations opportunity to meet members of the public and present the library's story.

## TAPPING COMMUNITY SOURCES FOR GIFTS AND GRANTS

Community residents and businesses have responded to library appeals when they've had a specified goal or program objective. Donations have ranged from the price of one book to the full cost of program printing and production.

### Matching Grants

The Tucson (Arizona) Public Library funds many of its programs through matching grants. The library obtains allocations from the Arizona Commission on the Arts and Humanities matched by contributions from its Friends, private foundations, a local community college or a local community service organization. About $4,000 is raised annually from matching grants for library programming.

These funds support such programs as a writers workshop, performances by area theatrical, opera, symphony and dance organizations as well as lectures dealing with aspects of "The Southwest Story," a look at the history, culture, heritage, and natural world of the desert.

Grants pay for program printing, publicity, space rental when necessary, and other incidental expenses. Speakers normally donate their time and services.

## Phonathon

The supporters of the Darien (Connecticut) Public Library raised more than $70,000 toward a new building by holding a phonathon. Scheduled over six evenings, participants called 1,500 prospective donors throughout the community soliciting contributions. When telephone volunteers came to the library to work, the library provided sandwiches and soft drinks.

In addition to the funds raised through the phonathon, some $600,000 was contributed through special gifts.

## Memorial Books

The San Marino (California) Public Library expands its collection of special books through a Memorial Book program. The librarian purchases a variety of attractive, illustrated volumes on such topics as travel and gardening, which are maintained in the office.

Community patrons can purchase the books — at the library's costs — in memory of a friend or relative, to commemorate a birthday, birth, anniversary or other special occasion, or as a gift. All books, with special bookplates designating "in honor of" the individual named, are added to the permanent collection.

In the case of gifts, the books are wrapped and delivered to the recipient who can read them first, and then return them to the library's regular collection.

About 150 books are sold annually, freeing some $1500 for other acquisitions. Inventory is added as new titles of interest are published.

## Funds From Student Service Clubs

Students at Montgomery Blair High School (Silver Spring, Maryland), have funded the purchase of books, study carrels and plants for the library media center. Working through their service clubs, high schoolers held bake sales, car washes and book fairs. One group, which participated on television's "It's Academic," contributed its prize money to the library for purchase of plants to decorate the renovated media center.

Student efforts bring the library media center between $100 and $150 each year.

## Buy a Brick

About 100 "signature bricks" have been sold by the

Toledo-Lucas County Public Library (Ohio) to support the main library's lawn beautification project, which is part of the city's downtown revitalization plan. The granite bricks will form a "Walk on the Bright Side" walkway and bear the name, actual signature or service mark of the donor, or an in memorium message. Businesses buy bricks for $200 each, individuals for $100. One brick was purchased by children who raised $108 in small donations to honor the school mascot, an eagle. Brick sales have raised about $15,000 towards the cost of landscaping.

## SPECIAL EVENTS

Holiday, seasonal or activity related events have proven successful for many friends groups. Many of these lend themselves to duplication in ensuing years and develop a following which can increase with each event.

### Fashion Shows

Professionally-modeled spring or fall fashions have been a popular fundraiser for Friends of the Hingham (Massachusetts) Public Library. Held biennially since 1973, the fashion preview is coordinated with a top local retailer with narration supplied by the store's fashion consultant or the modeling agency.

Lunch is catered, with champagne donated by local distributors.

Tickets for the three-hour event, including lunch, have ranged form $7.50 the first year to $15 this year and net the Library between $1,500 and $2,000.

## Haunted House

An old house slated for demolition, lumber, and paint helped the Owatonna (Minnesota) Public Library earn $200 and enabled residents to share in a fun Halloween haunted house promotion. The house, owned by the library, was prepared for the four-day event with lumber and black paint donated by area businesses. Jaycee volunteers helped with decorating and selling tickets. Local actors and community group guides operated the house for four evenings and two matinees.

The haunted house "tour" was part of the community's annual "Pumpkin Days" celebration.

## Readers Marathon

About 1100 Philadelphia fifth through eighth graders participated in a month-long readers marathon cosponsored by the Friends of the Free Library of Philadelphia and community school district and teachers' associations. Children signed up sponsors at pledges of 10¢ and up per book read; one child also sponsored himself at 1¢ per book.

Suggested reading corners were set up in the library for participants' use, and parents verified that books were read. Any child completing at least one book and obtaining at least one sponsor was eligible for prizes, which were given away through a drawing at a party hosted by the Friends. Donated by businesses and individuals, prizes ranged from a trip to Copenhagen for a child and one adult to family starter libraries, cameras, and book purchase certificates.

About $12,000 was raised for children's programming at the Free Library branches and other marathons are planned for the future.

## Arts and Crafts Festival

A day long arts and crafts festival is an enjoyable fundraising activity for the Jenkintown, Pennsylvania, Public Library. Sponsored for the third year by the library's Associates, the festival includes exhibits by 100 to 150 arts and crafts makers selected by jury; free entertainment supplied by local musicians, ballet students and a karate studio; a variety of food concessions operated by area restaurants and the library. The Associates also sell specially-designed T-shirts.

Ads soliciting artist participation are scheduled in appropriate magazines, local newspapers, and the Philadelphia media.

During the festival, judges view the exhibits and select winners in various categories and ribbons are awarded. Afterwards, a wine and cheese reception is held for all winners.

Exhibitors pay $20 to participate; concessionaires pay 20% of the day's gross, and local merchants also contribute toward the library fund. The festival nets between $4,000 and $5,000.

Between 10,000 and 20,000 people turn out for the festival each year, giving the sponsors a wide audience for promoting the library and the work of the Associates.

## A SPORTING CHANCE FOR LIBRARIES

Local sports figures or sporting events can be a focal point for library fundraising activities. Sporting events can include spectator or participatory activities depending on the interests of the community.

### Kentucky Derby Party

Friends of the St. John the Baptist Parish Public Library, LaPlace, Louisiana, held a Kentucky Derby Party for the library. The group rented horse race films along with straw hats and arm bands to give the party a racetrack flavor.

Local distributors contributed alcoholic beverages which the Friends sold at a cash bar tended by volunteers. A door prize was given away and other donated items were auctioned off.

Tickets were sold at $5 per person — printing was donated by a local businessman. Net profit for the event was about $200.

### #1 Library Fund

Indiana University is noted for many things — including a championship basketball team. Several years ago, coach Bob Knight and the Indiana University Foundation developed a winning idea in support of the University Library: a "#1 Library Fund" drive.

A promotional brochure *What's #1 in My Book* was created, with much of the text provided by Knight. Full-page ads appeared in every home basketball game program calling attention to the need for increasing the library's book budget and building the collection and professional staff.

Knight appeared in a videotape televised during the first IU halftime show during the promotion period and talked about the library fund on his own weekly TV program.

The appeal was sent to alumni and friends of the University and has raised more than $25,000.

## Road Race

Alabama's Huntsville-Madison County Public Library sponsored a 5-mile road race through downtown Huntsville. The race drew 153 runners (at $3 per adult entrant, $1 for students) and several individuals who joined in a "half mile fun run." McDonald's cooperated by distributing flyers, providing drinks for the runners, and hamburger certificates for winners.

Planned as an annual National Library Week event, the race started at the library and drew many individuals who had not previously visited the facility. The event netted $136, used to increase the library's collection of books on running.

# Appendix A

## A CHECKLIST FOR PLANNING

☐ Start your planning well enough in advance to allow for generating interest but not too for in advance to discourage committee workers and potential participants.

☐ Check with other groups and governmental agencies to make sure that the library's fundraiser is not in competition with other popular activities or coming at the same time as other fundraisers.

☐ Select an event that will have the broadest appeal for the community, or one that fits with a current popular trend.

☐ Set up a committee of dedicated volunteers to take the pressure off the library staff. Assign a library staff member who can serve as liaison between the program committee and the library.

☐ Committee members should be assigned specific responsibilities for the project — i.e., ticket sales, arrangements, printing, publicity, donation collections for sales, mailings, or food.

☐ Set *realistic* goals for your fundraising activities both in terms of attendance and anticipated profit. Over ambitious plans might result in disappointment for workers and participants.

☐ Set up a budget for the project with allocations for necessary expenditures. Determine the sources for the seed money. Will this come from the library? The Friends Group? Contributions from civic or service sponsors?

☐ Select a place, time and date for the event. Plan for a "rain date" for an outside event or for an alternative location.

☐ Develop a mailing list of potential contributors, community leaders to be invited or lend support, past supporters, and foundations or funds to be tapped.

☐ Start small. A successful first event will generate interest, volunteers, and participation for future events. A reachable goal — when attained or surpassed — encourages participants to work even harder next time.

☐ Don't overmeet. Have the full committee meet periodically to update the entire group on various stages in the progress of the activity. However, the committee works better when the subgroups can proceed without the necessity to hold reporting sessions.

☐ Utilize individual specialties so that creative people work on the development of graphics; good sales people sell, and organizers coordinate the work of others. They'll be happier and more will be accomplished.

☐ Plan an evaluation session following the completion of the fundraising event. This will identify problem areas for the future as well as provide guidance on ways to improve future efforts.

☐ Involve the community and call on resources to help with donations of items for sales as well as financial contributions; access to supplies, and services not available in the library (manpower for distribution of flyers, printing, media for publicity assistance, promotion of the library event through other groups).

☐ Set up interviews with a library or committee spokesperson for newspaper stories on what the fundraising activities will mean to the community. Book appearances by such spokesperson on public affairs programs on the electronic media.

☐ Give short presentations or speeches before community groups such as the Kiwanis, Elks, PTA, and Rotarians asking their support or endorsement of the effort.

Possible Community Resources:

☐ Graphics studios, artists or creative people at advertising agencies for assistance with program, flyer, ticket, and poster design.

☐ Printers for paper and production services either at reduced rates or as a contribution to the library.

☐ Boy Scouts, Girl Scouts, and high school service clubs for assistance in distributing materials.

☐ Banks, department stores, and other retail outlets to underwrite aspects of the project or to display promotional materials, handouts, and flyers.

☐ Utilities for inclusion of flyers in their monthly statement mailings.

☐ State arts agencies who can serve as cosponsors of cultural activities.

☐ Professional societies, civic groups, and service clubs who can assist with volunteers and financing.

☐ Shopping center management who might make a mall or auditorium available should the library have insufficient space.

☐ Grocery stores or chains who might make bags available for book sales, arts and crafts sales, or other similar events. They, too, could be contacted for publicizing the fundraising event.

☐ Newspapers, radio, and television stations for publicity on the event — before, during, and after. Radio and television stations have "public service" time available for such activities.

# Appendix B

## SELECTED RESOURCES

A. General Fundraising

THE COMPLETE FUND RAISING GUIDE,
by Howard R. Mirkin
Public Service Materials Center, 1972.

A useful general discussion with particularly helpful how-to chapters on business and employee campaigns, memorial giving, direct mail, house-to-house solicitations, and special events.

FUND RAISING: A PROFESSIONAL GUIDE,
by William R. Cumerford
Ferguson E. Peters Company, 1978.

Written by a professional consultant, this book shows how to organize a full-scale fundraising campaign, step-by-step. This would be very useful for a library planning a major campaign, including corporate and foundation gifts. Everyone can profit from Cumer-

ford's premise, "People give to promising programs —
not to needy institutions."

THE GRASSROOTS FUNDRAISING BOOK: HOW
TO RAISE MONEY IN YOUR COMMUNITY,
by Joan Flanagan
Swallow Press, 1977.

This is a useful, step-by-step guide to all kinds of fundraisers. The author studied 150 organizations in some
25 communities — rural to urban — and came up with
detailed how-to's for everything from *Benefits for Be-
ginners* — book or plant sales, coffees, haunted house,
movies, pot luck suppers, and raffles — to *The Big Time*
— ad books, antique or art fairs, carnivals, concerts,
casino nights, marathons, movie premiers, and tennis
tournament. In between she also discusses auctions,
bazaars, celebrity lectures, cocktail parties, cookbooks, dances, house tours, luncheons, and theatre
parties. *And* she reviews the basics of direct mail, corporate giving, business help, and canvassing. A helpful basic for community fundraisers. Bibliography.

HANDBOOK OF SPECIAL EVENTS FOR NON-
PROFIT ORGANIZATIONS: TESTED IDEAS FOR
FUND RAISING AND PUBLIC RELATIONS,
by Edwin Reisinger Leibert and Bernice E. Sheldon
Association Press, 1972.

This book emphasizes basic planning and suggests key
questions to help planners clarify goals and the best
way to meet them. Using short case studies and para-

graph "experience reports," the book shows what many groups have done and offers a base for brainstorming sessions libraries might want to hold. Special events are discussed by type, including opening events for fundraising campaigns, charity balls, fashion shows, art exhibits, bazaars, fairs, house tours, theater benefits, and the like. Sample programs, announcements, posters, and invitations illustrate how-to's for effective events.

KRC FUND RAISER'S MANUAL: A GUIDE TO PERSONALIZED FUND RAISING,
by Paul Blanshard, Jr.
KRC Development Council 1974.

Written by a professional fundraiser, this book emphasizes the person-to-person approach for all kinds of fundraising activities libraries might try. It is aptly subtitled "A How-to-Do-It Manual on Capital Fund Campaigning, Special Project Fund Raising, Annual Giving, Deferred Giving and Foundation Grantsmanship."

MAKING THE MOST OF SPECIAL EVENTS,
by Harold N. Weiner.
Public Relations Society of America 1977.

This 20-page brochure is part of a series "Managing Your Public Relations: Guidelines for Nonprofit Organizations." It is basic and straightforward information which would be helpful for library directors.

MONEY RAISING ACTIVITIES FOR COMMU-
NITY GROUPS: A 'FUNDS AND FUN' GUIDE FOR
AGENCY AND COMMUNITY FAIRS, BAZAARS,
AND OTHER MONEY RAISING EVENTS,
by Virginia W. Musselman
Association Press, 1969.

The title pretty much says it all; this is a helpful guide,
with particularly good sections on organizing committees and other volunteer workers. Library fundraising
planners might find the "Twenty-Seven Once-a-Year
Events" helpful for getting creative juices going. This
is a how-to book, full of "shoulds." It is very basic and
can be a good beginning.


NONPROFIT ORGANIZATION HANDBOOK: A
GUIDE TO FUND RAISING, GRANTS, LOBBY-
ING, MEMBERSHIP BUILDING, PUBLICITY AND
PUBLIC RELATIONS,
by Patricia V. Gaby and Daniel M. Gaby
Prentice-Hall, 1979.

In a convenient looseleaf format, this thorough guide
covers all aspects of fundraising and would be particularly useful for libraries making an across-the-board
assessment of financial needs and alternative sources
for funds, including grants and major gift campaigns.
The sections on special events, mailings, volunteer
training and supervision, and creative public relations
are excellent. The book takes a step-by-step approach
to every specific aspect of fundraising which it covers.

## B. Library Fundraising and Public Relations

THE ABC'S OF LIBRARY PROMOTION,
by Steve Sherman
Scarecrow, 1971.

Concerned primarily with the how-to's of library public relations, this title is not geared specifically to fundraising activities. However, the book contains helpful detailed information on certain aspects of a full-fledged fundraising program.

AMERICAN LIBRARIES "Money" Issue,
November/December, 1977.

Case studies on various fundraising programs include successful bond issues at Portland-Multnomah County Library (Oregon), Atlanta Public Library, and Marion (Ohio) Public Library. There is also a useful glossary *The Lingo of Library Finance* and information on how to get grants, federal funding for libraries and academic library budget techniques.

EXTERNAL FUND RAISING IN ARL LIBRARIES.
SPEC (Systems and Procedures Exchange Center)
Kit #48 from the Office of University Library Management Studies, Assoiation of Research Libraries, 1978.

This kit concentrates on grants but would be useful for all types of libraries interested in developing funding through grantsmanship.

FUNDING ALTERNATIVES FOR LIBRARIES,
by Patricia Senn Breivik and E. Burr Gibson
American Library Association, 1979.

A primer for alternative funding sources for libraries, this book compiles papers from a 1976 fundraising workshop at the Pratt Institute Graduate School of Library and Information Science. The authors look at the planning process — how to decide on funding alternatives and prepare to pursue them — and outline various approaches in-depth. These include annual fund and capital campaigns, direct mail solicitation, special events, government funding, lobbying and foundation funding. Three case studies illustrate the how-tos of library fundraising programs at Portland, Maine Public Library, The Kresge Library of Oakland University and the Performing Arts Research Center of the New York Public Library. A good, thorough basic resource.

THE HARRIED LIBRARIAN'S GUIDE TO
PUBLIC RELATIONS SOURCES,
by Marian S. Edsall
The Coordinated Library Information Program, Inc., 1976.

A useful PR resource, this book contains information on everything a library fundraiser could ever need. Included is a good short bibliography of fundraising and special events programs, and friends activities.

LIBRARY PR NEWS,
Library Education Institute

A bimonthly devoted specifically to library PR programs and ideas, this publication can be helpful for library fundraisers who understand the relationship of financial support and public relations.

PR FOR PENNIES:
LOW-COST LIBRARY PUBLIC RELATIONS,
by Virginia Van Wynen Baeckler
Sources, 1978.

A useful booklet with good ideas and practical how-to's for library PR, this title includes good graphics that show what other libraries have accomplished.

PREPARE! THE LIBRARY PUBLIC
RELATIONS RECIPE BOOK,
Compiled and edited by Irene E. Moran
Prepared by the Public Relations Section, Library Administration and Management Association, American Library Association, 1978.

A basic and handy compendium of ideas and procedures to strengthen any library's relations with its public. Many of the topics will come up in fundraising projects, and there is also a good section on "legislative tips" and a good bibliography of PR material.

PROJECTING A POSITIVE IMAGE
THROUGH PUBLIC RELATIONS,
by Cosette Kies
American Library Association, 1978.

Though not directed at fundraising activities, this booklet discusses the basics which any school library fundraiser should consider.

PUBLIC RELATIONS FOR LIBRARIES:
ESSAYS IN COMMUNICATIONS TECHNIQUES,
Edited by Allan Angoff
Greenwood Press No. 5, Contributions in Librarianship and Information Science, 1973.

Consisting of a dozen essays on public relations in specific library settings, from metropolitan libraries to children's room, an academic library to a suburban library system, this title contains useful how-to's but mentions fundraising only incidentally.

PUBLIC RELATIONS FOR PUBLIC LIBRARIES:
CREATIVE PROBLEM SOLVING,
by Betty Rice
Wilson, 1972.

The basic premise, as the first chapter explains, is that "Public Relations is a Way of Life." Chapters on special events, programs, and bond issues are of particular help for developing fundraisers.

PUBLIC RELATIONS: INFORMATION SOURCES,
by Alice Norton
Gale Research, 1970.

This in-depth bibliographic resource has particularly useful sections on attitudes and marketing research, publicity, special events, fundraising, and corporate support.

## C. Friends of Libraries

A DIRECTORY OF FRIENDS OF LIBRARIES
GROUPS IN THE UNITED STATES,
compiled by Sandy Dolnick
American Library Association, 1978.

This 297-page spiralbound book lists some 2100 public and academic Friends groups. This is a basic listing, with no in-depth materials about Friends activities or fundraisers. However, it would be useful for library planners interested in talking with nearby groups before undertaking their own activities.

FRIENDS OF THE LIBRARIES
ORGANIZATIONS,
SPEC (Systems and Procedures Exchange Center)
Kits #6 and 22, from the Office of University Library Management Studies, Association of Research Libraries, 1974 and 1977.

These kits consist mainly of sample materials from

various friends groups and make a handy one-stop source for ideas on developing such organizations.

**FRIENDS OF THE LIBRARY NATIONAL NOTEBOOK,**
American Library Association.

A quarterly newsletter featuring articles of interest to Friends groups, reports of activities sponsored by groups around the country, notes on books, booklets and other how-to or promotional materials sold by Friends groups, and book reviews relevant to Friends.

**BOOK SALE MANUAL,**
The Friends of the San Francisco Public Library, 1975.

**BOOK SALE MANUAL,**
by Gloria Comingore and Pat Petersen, the Friends of the Torrance, California Library, 1976.

**EXTENSION KIT,**
The Friends of California Libraries, 1973.

Useful how-to section includes bond issues, gifts and donations, and used book sales.

FIND OUT WHO YOUR FRIENDS ARE: A
PRACTICAL MANUAL FOR THE FORMATION
OF LIBRARY SUPPORT GROUPS,
The Friends of the Free Library of Philadelphia,
1978.

LET'S BE FRIENDS,
The Friends of Libraries in Oklahoma, 1979.

This is a handbook for organizing local Friends of
the library groups. It is geared specifically to Oklahoma friends, but the basics are the same
everywhere. Though this 32-page spiralbound booklet does not go into detail on fundraising projects, it
would be helpful for any fledgling Friends organization. Includes a short bibliography of Friends resources.

A MANUAL OF SUGGESTIONS AND
PROBLEMS FOR LIBRARIANS AND
FRIENDS ORGANIZATIONS,
The Friends of Hennepin County (Edina, Min-
nesota) Library, 1979.


D. Community Profile

LIBRARY TRENDS "Community Analysis and
Libraries" issue, January, 1976.
Larry Earl Bone, Issue Editor.

A thorough, wide-ranging introduction to the subject

of community analysis, from the rationale to the results. As Allie Beth Martin stated in her overview article, "Each library must develop its own goals, determined by the uniqueness of each community or institution . . . community analysis on the part of the library is critical, and must be a constant process."

The fifteen contributions to this State of the Art report include a bibliography and much material of use to library planners considering community analysis or user profiles as part of their financial planning process.

LITERACY AND THE NATION'S LIBRARIES,
by Helen Huguenor Lyman
American Library Association, 1977.

This book contains material on community assessment. Library planners contemplating this process will find pp. 33 – 44 and pp. 139 – 140 particularly useful. These sections introduce the rationale and procedures for community assessment. They also offer checklists of areas to consider and resources for compiling information.

LOCAL POWER AND THE
COMMUNITY LIBRARY,
by Edward N. Howard
American Library Association, 1978.

A look at the power structure in most communities. This book describes the various community groups

— governmental and independent — which affect and effect decision-making concerning libraries. This is interesting reading for all public library planners who want to understand the political structure in which they operate.

MEASURING THE QUALITY OF
LIBRARY SERVICE: A HANDBOOK,
by M.G. Fancher Beeler and others.
Scarecrow Press, 1974.

A compilation of nearly 30 articles on measuring techniques and how to determine recommendations based on research. This book includes an annotated bibliography on gathering statistics on a national scale and on the planning process in individual libraries.

# Appendix C

## 'OF FRIENDS AND FUNDS'

The following list of fundraising projects was compiled by the State Library of Florida based on questionnaires to all Florida Friends of libraries groups. Reprinted with permission, it provides a sample of the variety of community-based fundraisers libraries can try.

Funds from Deferred Giving

Endowments
Estate & property donations
Investing cash
Memorial fund
Scholarships
Trust funds
Will remembrance

Funds from Donations

Ask for it
Auxiliary

Blue Chip Stamps
Business and industry
Cashing promotional coupons
Churches
Contact civic groups for sponsors or volunteers
Contracts for services
Donations from sponsors
Door-to-door solicitation
Foundations
Grantee fund drives
Grants
Inter-agency fundraising
Local governments
Mailouts
Percentage receipts in stores, bars, restaurants
Radio & TV Station auctions
RSVP telethon, radiothon, walkathon, bicyclethon
Service clubs
Soliciting private business for goods and services
Sponsors to adopt volunteers/program
Trading stamps
Unions

## Funds through Entertainment

A Day at the Races
Battle of the Bands
Beauty Contest for Seniors
Benefit dinner/dance
Bingo
Block party

Card parties
Carnival
Coordinated benefits
Cruises
Dances, socials, garden parties
Dinners with guest speakers
Donkey ball games
Dramas
Fashion Show
Film festivals
Fishing Tournaments
Golden follies
Horseshoe pitching
Lectures, concerts
Luau
Musicals
Plays
Potlucks
Recognitions
Rodeos
Senior follies
Sponsor special interest projects
Sports Tournaments
Street dances
Style Shows
   A. Using senior needlecraft
   B. Straight style show
Talent Show
Testimonial dinner
Theatre parties

Theatre, race track proceeds for "premier on
   opening night"
Theatrical productions
Tours
Tractor Pulls
Wine & cheese tasting party

## Funds through Political Change

Bond issues
Campaign (sponsors)
Change ACTION policies so can get more dollars
City and County Commissioners
Formal presentations to government agencies
Go to legislators through state agencies you may be
   serving on
Legislation for a special tax
Letters to Legislature
Library Day in the courthouses of local governments
Library Day in the legislature
National Action
Revenue Sharing

## Funds through Sale of Goods

Antique bazaar
"Artistic" hot dog sale
Attic Auction
Auctions
Auto resale
Bake sales

Bazaars
Book n' Snack Shop
Bumper sticker sales
Candy sales
Christmas card or tree sales
Craft classes — find a sponsor and sell the crafts
Crafts by seniors
Dutch Auctions
Farmers Market
Flea Fair
Flea Market
Flower sales
Food Fair
Friends logo jewelry sale
Garage sales
"Gray Power" button sale
Make and sell cards for seasonal occasions
Plant boutique
Recycling bottles, cans, newspapers
Refunds on empty bottles
Rumage sales
Senior citizen tag day
Senior craft boutique
Swap meets
Thrift and gift shops
Thrift shop of convalescent hospital —
    RSVP gets percentage
Ticket commissions
Tupperware parties
Used book sale
White elephant sales

Funds through Sale of Services

Auxiliary
Car washes
Catering service
Contracted special programs
Handyman
Junior Friends workdays
Memberships
Radio advertising — RSVP gets percentage
Rent-a-grandmother, grandfather, or kid
Senior dating service
Speakers Bureau
Sponsor special interest projectrs
Sustaining memberships
Telephone answering

We gratefully acknowledge the cooperation and assistance of the staff and friends of the following libraries, without whom this book would not have been possible:

Alvin (Texas) Community College Library
Appleton (Wisconsin) Public Library
Baltimore County Public Library (Towson, Maryland)
Bemis Public Library (Littleton, Colorado)
Brandeis University Libraries (Waltham, Massachusetts)
Columbus (Ohio) Public Library
Dallas (Texas) Public Library
Darien (Connecticut) Public Library
Free Library of Philadelphia (Pennsylvania)
Hingham (Massachusetts) Public Library
Huntsville-Madison County (Alabama) Public Library
Indiana University Library (Bloomington, Indiana)
Jacksonville (Florida) Public Library
Jenkintown (Pennsylvania) Public Library
Johnson School of Technology (Scranton, Pennsylvania)
Ketchum/Sun Valley (Idaho) Community Library
Malcolm Love Library (San Diego, California, State University)
Marin Country Day School (Corte Madera, California)
McKinley Elementary School (Elkins Park, Pennsylvania)
Millard Library (Omaha, Nebraska)
Minneapolis (Minnesota) Public Library
Montgomery Blair High School (Silver Spring, Maryland)
New York (New York) Public Library
Oak Park (Illinois) Public Library
Oakville (Ontario, Canada) Public Library
Owatonna (Minnesota) Public Library
Public Library of Johnston County and Smithfield (North Carolina)
St. John the Baptist Parish Public Library (LaPlace, Louisiana)
Samford University Library (Birmingham, Alabama)
San Marino (California) Public Library
School-Community Resource Center (Wheaton, Illinois)
Toledo-Lucas County (Ohio) Public Library
Topeka West High School Library (Topeka, Kansas)
Tucson (Arizona) Public Library
Unionville Elementary School (Union County, North Carolina)
University of Houston (Texas) Libraries
University of Rochester (New York) Libraries